Change and the Teacher

THE PHILOSOPHY OF
A SOCIAL PHENOMENON

Forthcoming by Sandford Reichart

Teaching the Disadvantaged:

A PRACTICAL GUIDE

SANDFORD REICHART

Coordinator of MAT Programs AND

Associate Professor of Education

JOHN CARROLL UNIVERSITY

Change and the Teacher

THE PHILOSOPHY OF
A SOCIAL PHENOMENON

Thomas Y. Crowell Company, Inc.

NEW YORK   ESTABLISHED   1834

*To my mother who taught me
that as the seasons change
each unknown can become but
another time of beauty, and
to my sister who shared so
much of that beauty with me.*

Contents

Contents

Introduction

I teach. I've seen changes come to teaching and expect to see more. I know what it is to have to teach sex to a fifth grade class and wonder how you're going to say that vagina is vagina and not a triangle and that penis is penis and not an arrow. I've had to face the so-called new math when I didn't even know the old. I saw the Belgian Congo disappear from the old map and reappear with its challenge to learn about a different country, a different geography, a different history. I've seen Africa change and my books become old overnight and my preparation obsolete—and been faced with becoming obsolete myself.

I state this not to brag, for where I have taken one step forward I might have taken ten. I state this as I would toss my credentials upon a table. Why? Because I care and because caring encompasses the desire to share. The teaching profession is an art and we cannot afford to allow it to disappear into mediocrity because change threatens our security and anesthetizes our ability to teach.

It is not a question of survival. If percentages are to be reckoned with, probably eighty percent of the teachers will go right on teaching no matter what changes take place. Come intellectual fire, come racial storm, come spiritual upheaval, somehow the majority will stay bound to the profession. It is not a matter of survival, but how we survive and whether or not it is worth surviving—worth it to us and to the profession. There are times and places and circumstances in life that make survival alone enough, but hardly ever in education—not if it means any more than mere breadwinning and a guaranteed retirement fund.

Change will threaten and a few will escape to marriage and home, a few will find a more tempting career, a few will accept any substitute, but most will go on teaching. Certainly, we can sit back on our laurels and bide our time until retirement, or live for the day we can get a transfer, or we can do something about what we are where we are—because places and events may change, but our role in them won't unless *we* change—not tomorrow, not next week, but now!

Facing change is seldom easy for teachers, especially the gentle, the meek, the sensitive, but then neither is facing life with worthiness and courage easy—both challenge. Some of us may never face change with the spirit of a hero or the enthusiasm of an evangelist; some of us may never be bold human beings or bold teachers, or bold anything! But how do we know? How do we know what we may achieve until we have the courage to try, to start? And if we only step up the ladder from C to B − , at the least that is something, and far more than if we had never lifted even one foot.

There is no question about it, change is here and we can walk with it or be left behind it—or we might be blessed enough to walk ahead of it. Let us begin by trying to understand it.

The Roman poet Ovid, who died about seventeen years after the birth of Christ, left *The Metamorphoses* to the legions who were to follow him. In Book Fifteen of this great work, Ovid gave us as majestic a concept of change as is to be found in all the literature of the world.

All things are in a state of flux, and everything is brought into being with a changing nature. Time itself flows on in constant motion, just like a river. For neither the river nor the swift hour can stop its course; but as wave is pushed on by wave, and as each wave comes in both pressed on and itself presses the wave in front, so time both flees and follows and is ever new. For that which once existed is no more, and that which was not has come to be; and so the whole round of motion is gone through again.

In *The Faerie Queene* Edmund Spenser spoke of "the ever-whirling wheel of Change," while Tennyson referred to "the ringing groves of change," and Thoreau said that "things do not change; we change."

Throughout the ages, man has observed that things do not remain static. Past events become blurred by the scenes of the present which, in turn, are destined to become like those blurred yesterdays, drifting into the dreams and anticipation of moments yet to come. Nothing remains static. Man has known throughout his history that this moment, this time may be suspended in the space of a dream but that it, as with all moments, must move on. And in the moving onward, *tempora mutantur, et nos mutamur in illis.* "The times are changing, and we are changing in them."

What is change? Can it be put upon a slide and analyzed under a microscope? Not likely, for it will remain always as a quality, as something that became while the becoming was not conscious. Yet, it is the conviction of this book that we must make it conscious, that we must attempt to control the becoming, that we must make of this quality a recognizable experience that can stand apart, that we can affect while it is effecting.

Change can mean "to alter by substituting something else for, by giving up for something else." It can mean "to put or take another or others in place of," or "to cause to pass from one state to another; to convert." It might mean "to render something essentially different from what it was, even to loss of identity."

But Webster is not the answer, not for the teacher. And this book is for the teacher. It is for the teacher who is, the one who is yet to be, for all those who are interested in teaching, in education, in growth, and in being more alive while living more analytically. It is for all in many interrelated disciplines who see its meaning and can translate it into relevance.

This is a book dedicated to change. Its sole purpose is that of presenting a way of looking at change, a way of dealing with some of its issues and grasping some of its implications.

I do not intend to say that my way of dealing with the problem is the only way. Rather, I offer it as one possible alternative approach in the earnest hope that it may communicate my belief that unless teachers understand the significance of change they cannot deal effectively with the profound challenges of our dynamic age.

With gratitude to my editor and friend, Stanley Rinehart, it is impossible to look back over the years when the idea for this book was germinating without being deeply grateful for my association with such steadfast friends as Dr. Miriam Goldberg, Frank G. Jennings, Hannah Levin, Dr. A. Harry Passow, and Dr. Abraham Tannenbaum; but without my cousin Bascom Biggers III, his energies and encouragement, this book would have remained a thought waiting for completion.

1. About the Teacher and Change

In the aftermath of birth and death, the quality that is change seems almost an entity unto itself. It is as though we can taste it, touch it, hold it. The change we experience in our professional world is not always so apparent. Nevertheless, it is an ever present reality. Whether it comes abruptly or gradually, harshly or gently, we must face it, accept it, and understand it if we are to use it.

WHERE DOES CHANGE ORIGINATE?

St. Augustine wrote that we must "Trust the Past to the Mercy of God, the Present to His Love, the Future to His Providence." In a sense he was telling us that the three major change periods we know as past, present, and future are within the management province of God. Whether or not we accept this is a personal matter, but what is not personal is our acceptance of the fact that change itself is a natural phenomenon. Nothing is static. All things and all events have their moment of beginning, their antecedents, their evolution into other levels of development and expression, into other dimensions as they move on to other forms of energy, other uses. Even death may be viewed as another form of energy, not an ending but a change of condition, a change of form with a change of meaning.

In a professional sense, the teacher has too often replaced the God of St. Augustine with the ritualistic observance of tradition, has too often founded the actions of today only upon what was done yesterday, and thus has been detached from a futuristic attitude. Certainly the past should be a bedrock—but to stand upon to extend the grasp, not to sleep upon.

When a group of parents knocks at the classroom door and asks why some new technique for prenatally teaching the child to read has not been investigated, the teacher is apt to become defensively protective of status quo. "I am the educator," she may say. "And I have done this for hundreds of children all during the twenty-two years I have loved children and taught children," she may continue amidst the quivering of her upper lip. Or the teacher may be politely unmoved. "How terribly exciting that must be," she will say. "I hadn't heard about it. You say you read about it in the *Reader's Digest?* Well, I must get hold of that issue." Other teachers may do nothing but hope that this ugly specter will vanish as though it had never really appeared. Still other teachers may find the notion exciting and even rational yet limit their enthusiasm and exhaust their energies with, "Well, they may get that over there in the Weeping Lagoon School System, but we'll never get it here. That's the trouble with us. We don't get paid enough, we have too many children to teach, we have too much homework to correct. How can they expect us to take this on too?" And suddenly the issue of teaching the child to read prenatally is lost in the clouds of excuses and rationalizations that confuse so many educational discussions.

Change is a part of living. It makes for the birth of the new. It promises the renaissance of the old. It furrows the way with memories, leaving shadows of what has been and may appear to be no more. It is tradition moving toward innovation. Change is life. Change is death. It is being born. It is living. It is dying. In between it is sex and the expression of sex—and reproduction. It is adolescence—and menopause—and old age. It is here and now.

Change comes out of the interaction of people with the events they make, out of their desire to create with events even as they are occurring. We live within events, some being external to us, others being more immediate.

The teacher interacts with events on two main levels. There is the personal interaction with the many people and events that make up a private world. There is the public interaction with authority figures, peer colleagues, parents, and the students. On each of these levels and with each of the people involved, the teacher faces a kind of perpetual motion wherein the people make an event. A child urinates on the floor, a teacher sternly reprimands the child, a parent scolds the teacher for having made the child nervous, a principal supports the teacher in her disciplinary actions, a colleague tells the teacher that she had difficulty with the same parent, and the teacher's maiden Aunt Maude hearing the story reminds the teacher that she herself as a girl had to be defended for wetting her panties. And because of this event a response has to be made in the form of an action, and as a result of this action an interaction takes place and out of this interaction the creative process develops.

So John's misplaced urine does not remain as remote to the teacher as does perhaps the capture of the U.S.S. *Pueblo*. Instead, it becomes quite immediate and an immediate chain of responses is released in the form of actions, some of which are very creative. John cannot go on using the floor, so he is given psychological referral for testing. The teacher cannot go on being too stern so the principal promises that she will ask her to be a bit more subtle in her approach. The parent does go right on being upset and organizes a group of mothers into a work-study organization with a school psychologist as their major consultant, and dedicated to the problems of toilet training and its role in education. Aunt Maude who has successfully faced wet panties decides to take adult education courses that might one day lead to emergency teaching certification: she has plain common good sense and you just don't learn that out of any book.

So any one happening can lead to changes of all sorts and try as we will we cannot stop these happenings. Our lives are made up of such situations, conditions, events. We do not live in a vacuum with abstractions filling in the void. We live within events that happened, that are happening, that will happen. Living means that we interact with these events because they affect us and we respond. We accept some, we reject others. To some we are dispassionate, to others we are aroused. At times the events make us tranquil, at times they make us frenetic. Now we love, now we hate, and all is a part of our being, of what we are and of what we would like to be. Sometimes these events bore us with their routine—how dull that the parent-teacher meeting must always be on Thursday night! Sometimes they fill us with fear because they are unknown—are we really capable of supervising a student teacher? They are the events of our work world, our private world, the world of our dreams, the world of our despairs. But we do not sit back and allow them to overwhelm us when we are prepared to be an active part of the world. Rather we try to change them even while they are taking shape. For these events and our interaction with them are the inner core of existence leading to war, to chaos, to the civil rights revolution; leading to the Renaissance, the Reformation, the ecumenical movement in religion, the exploration of space; leading to all that is to come.

THE NEGATIVE RESPONSE TO CHANGE

Unfortunately, teachers as a group appear to most observers to lack the perspectives of long-range thinking. They do not look ahead to 1980 and probe those corridors of awesome mystery. They appear more here-and-now-oriented, more concerned with the immediacies of their present routines, present scheduling problems, present details of course study. However practical these concerns are, they should occupy but one part of the teacher's being. Another, larger part should place these matters in appropriate position relative to the effects the actions and activities of today will have upon the events of tomorrow. How many teachers ask "What relevancy does this lesson have to the days ahead?" How many see such relevancies? Or are they not apt to be more concerned with the apparent needs of the particular lesson at hand? The teachers who do not come by it naturally need to learn the posture of looking ahead for themselves and their students, of seeing long-range goals, of planning today with projections into the future. For example, not just how well is the student reading, but equally important, is he stimulated by comprehending the exciting and awesome reality that reading is a primary key to all knowledge? Are his motives, as well as his ability, directed toward the promise of the future?

Lacking this interest or ability, as the case may be, the teacher becomes an organism in danger of living in a cocoon, unaware or, worse yet, afraid of the metamorphosis that transforms it into another state of being. Teachers have been caught with their courses of study down more than once. On one occasion the ogre of programmed learning sprang out at them. At another time the computer breathed forth its electronic fires before the embers of educational television had cooled. In the wake of such "monsters" all too many teachers perceive change as a foreboding interlocutor who poses a threat, who casts a doubt over what is being done and attempts to modulate what ought to be done. Rather than welcoming the possibility of the unknown as a likely alternative able to present a positive yield or shield of support, the teacher is apt to reject the unknown because it is unknown and by doing so leave unexplored many exciting avenues of curriculum and instruction, leave themselves instead of one step forward, two steps behind when the next area of change unfolds. Why learn the principles and uses of the program, the computer, or the television? "It will never *replace* us," the innovation-breakers say. "They'll see we are better. Besides," they rationalize," others will learn what to do with it, test its so-called importance, show up its weaknesses. I'll just wait until it's proved."

The teachers are too apt to perceive change as a break in their routine. And that which does not conform to the pattern of their habituated activity is all too apt to be viewed with suspicion or rejected outright. Only recently I had a teacher tell me, "No one will ever change my algebra periods from forty minutes of time every day of every week. Less time is too little—more is too much. And they need it every day." When I asked what if everyone does not need to take algebra someday, the teacher shouted back, "Never! *Everyone* needs algebra. It has always been that way and always will! That is, *here* it will. I don't know what they do in Russia."

THE CHALLENGE AND THE INSPIRATION
OF CHANGE

Not all teachers view change this way. Some are able to see it as a challenge, for that is what it is. It allows an inquiry into the new—an exploration seeking new meanings and new relationships. It may be viewed as a search or a quest. Man has not shirked this possibility: whether as the German critic Lessing devoted to the search, or as the Man of La Mancha pursuing the impossible dream, the quest has been a beacon lighting untraveled byways for many a journeyer throughout many an age.

You cannot become the traveler along the unknown road and remain as you were before. Along the way a metamorphosis occurs — you learn to use yourself differently and become different. You learn that as the signposts change, you change to capture their meanings. As the panorama shifts before your eyes, your attitudes adjust to take it in. You learn that we do not ourselves remain static in a world that moves. You discover that we meet the challenge through an expansion of our physical and mental capacities within the potential given us. And you learn that unused potential withers.

The use of this potential to greater fulfillment is our challenge. The use of ourselves in relating to all the changing patterns about us is our challenge. The making of a friend within the uncertainty of the unfamiliar is our challenge.

While working with a religious community I experienced how exciting the untraveled byways can be. The Sisters of this order had been faced with the problem of a decreasing enrollment and had come to realize that some drastic educational program would have to be designed if their school was not to close. Faced with so grave a possibility, their initial modest attempts at change came to be viewed by them as not dynamic enough to meet so overpowering a confrontation. Their plan had been to add some more time to some of the class periods of seniors by combining certain subjects: the plan they ended up with involved all the classes, all the class periods, and all the students.

Whereas in their initial approach to a strange path they had been filled with fear of the unknown roads, they now stood fast and stilled their pounding hearts with the energy of thinking. As one Sister said,

"Big. Stupendous." And it came as a revelation to them that they had to take the step of admitting that problems would exist but that nothing would be too formidable if they meant to resolve the obstacles. When their educational content faced challenge because of the schedule, they said, "Let's commit ourselves to the education we want and then work out the details." As they moved deeper and deeper into their commitment, they came more and more to work together, and their schedule rather than being a separator resulted in a type of cooperation rarely seen.

At the end of just one day of work, after nine hours of straight deliberation, the Sisters felt that their strangeness with the challenge had vanished. They had become campaign companions and been changed, even as their educational program was changed, by committing a dying school to plans for renewal.

Life is filled with such changes and it is the change that challenges us. The wonder of it all is that the change and the challenge become the inspiration that fills us with awe, that catapults us into action. Out of such inspiration man has risen to his finest moments.

WHAT CHANGES FACE THE TEACHER?

Since the teacher is a part of the world, he becomes part of all the changes within that world. These may be viewed as twofold, the macrocosmic conditions of living and those situational to being a teacher. Although they are related, the teacher is more apt to be concerned with those that are situational. Yet the macrocosmic conditions are generic to the human state. Whether conscious of them or not, the teacher is the recipient of the impact of all the forces surrounding the School. If there is a change in the life expectancy of man, the teacher is affected. A new wave of public concern over the population explosion affects the teacher as does an emergent change in attitude over morality, or an experiment that achieves the growth of a living cell in a test tube. Man's need to create within his environment, to interpret it differently, to modify its course, to control its dynamics, to probe its mysteries—all of this adds up to an influence upon the teacher. Why? Because for every question that is asked and every answer that is formulated, something more comes to be known about the world, something more comes to be known about life, something more comes to be added to the evidence that explains who we are, why we are, where we are going, and how we will get there. Every time man learns more, every time he analyzes more deeply, with every changing nuance he brings to his understanding of his world, the teacher is affected.

The pioneer attempts at heart transplant are certainly not immediate to the teacher. They are happening in South Africa or at Stanford to someone unknown. But such attempts must become part of the teacher's knowledge, part of his philosophical tone. To the science teacher certainly—but what if one is not a science teacher? Surely there are implications in heart transplants to man's understanding of himself and the world in which he lives, challenges to our emotions and ability to express empathy, to communicate with our dimensions of spirituality, our search for greater humanity through learning. Most certainly, whether or not a part of the subject field of the teacher, such attempts bring something new into the world and because of this something has changed. There will be no turning back for the researchers of heart transplant and teachers cannot turn back either. They have to be aware and have to translate that awareness into experience for the learners under their influence.

There is no place for the kind of teacher I observed saying to her English class of eighth graders, "Don't bring into this classroom those awful pictures of the blood and gore of that heart operation. There is a time and place for everything. This is English, not science." On the other hand, what of the General Science teacher who said to his class while I listened in, "I don't know about the transplant business. Haven't had time to read it yet. Why don't you do some extra credit reports on it? Make them two pages long and remember you get corrected on spelling in this class." If we don't know the answers, then, let's say so. There is no irrevocable sin in not being always on top of the moment, but we must not expect our students to compensate for our shortcomings. Even as we send them searching, we must go searching ourselves in the areas where change finds us wanting. And if our students, in their eager pursuit of knowledge, prod us beyond our self-imposed limits, we should not punish them with a grade at all in this area of their exploration—let alone mark them down for spelling! What creative mind caught up in the spirit of inspiration allows itself to be bogged down by such technicalities as spelling, grammar, and margins. These have their place, but not in the white heat of creative exploration, and never as an anchor to keep an inquiring spirit in tow behind us.

If the macrocosmic aspect of change often eludes the teacher, the situational changes seldom do, for these become part of the environment of the School and whatever the teacher's reaction, react he must. As society changes its style, as adjustments to problems are made, as new conventions are formulated, the School often responds by offering its interpretation through curriculum, through instruction, and through modifications in administrative apparatus. These become the changes that the teacher deals with by choice or through pressure. Whether it be a new approach to the teaching of mathematics or the use of television as a teaching aid, whether it be new content in social studies to deal with the war in Vietnam or the grouping of several teachers together to instruct as a team, the teacher feels these as changes in the situation that concerns him most. A different schedule, a different number of periods per week, the scheduling of training sessions: large or small, the teacher is attuned to such changes in the sensitive situation that is the School.

The teacher has to become quite accustomed to numerous operational changes, many of which relate to the personality of the principal. It is not uncommon to hear a weary teacher say at home something like, "Good grief, the new principal sure has changed a hell of a lot of stuff. He has us sending kids to the office *only* if they need counseling. Says it's our job if they need discipline. That wasn't old Thornton's way. He knew every kid in the school and they knew who was boss."

But then that is just one type of aggravating detail to which teachers grow accustomed but never resigned, and are seldom reluctant to bewail. There are changes in class schedules that sometimes occur the last minute, a new series of staff meetings that must be attended by all, a flock of transfer students dumped into the school without warning, a new textbook for World Geography, a change in the permanent record folder, and a brand new office of Special Services at the Board of Education—to name a few. Teachers do grow accustomed to such irritations as part of the liability of being a teacher.

They learn how to gripe when they are the recipients of all kinds of assaults, and they learn how to develop that good stiff upper lip that is prerequisite equipment for any martyr.

The problem with such pained resignation to situational innovations is that the teacher does not develop positive attitudes about change. Seeing it as something that upsets the applecart, as something to endure, something that is part of the hazards of the profession does not nurture healthy perceptions. *Seen as a villain, change cannot be used as a champion.* True, not all change is good, but all change is a possibility. Here is where the teacher needs help. If, in fact, change is part of the eternal order of things and if, in fact, the teacher is likewise a part of the eternal order, then these two parts just have to get together, have to work together as members of a team.

But teachers do not always work well together in any team sense. They often like the roost of the prima donna and find cooperative roundelays very hard to sing. As one of many examples, the dental profession is studying the adhesive properties of the barnacle and how the barnacle, which seems to be impervious to water, may have properties with implications for preventative dentistry. This is one of numerous cooperative ventures underway and countless dentists await the results and follow the course while waiting. It is difficult to find a comparable example of a group of teachers researching their profession in such a fashion. If they are practitioners they seem to be content with letting those who are remote from the classroom do the research for them. Then when the researchers to whom they have defaulted present proposals for change, these same teachers hide behind all the cliché excuses beginning and very often ending with, "It's all right for *them* to talk—they don't have to do it!"

We don't know whether or not barnacle research will come up with anything and whether or not it will ever become the kind of adhesive we might one day get in a dentist's chair—or want. But we do know one thing; in spite of the fact that there will always be some who will resist whatever is new, when the majority within a profession dedicated to serving mankind see some value in something new, they start taking the necessary steps to become a part of it or make it a part of them. This may be the answer for teachers. Perhaps we must come to see that we are part of a profession just as dedicated to serving mankind as, let's say dentistry, and perhaps we need to study change as a way of giving more service to mankind. Why not? The human being who comes under our guidance in the learning-growing process is certainly in a service relationship to us and perhaps we need to perceive change as something that might benefit him and therefore be mandatory to our teaching pattern. Whether or not we are comfortable becomes irrelevant—after all, teaching should not be our therapy.

THE TEACHER'S RESPONSIBILITY

More and more teachers will have to become less threatened by change. They will have to become so aware of change that it becomes second nature for them to analyze it as one fixed alternative among many. They will have to accept or reject change on the basis of rational behavior rather than upon emotional bias. Such an approach could result in teachers becoming leaders as they rightly should be by using change as something to create upon rather than having change control them through external pressures. Teachers should direct the course of change through the use of their trained minds and the development of abilities necessary to expose issues to dissection before plotting their direction.

Let us look, for example, at the time preceding the meteoric appearance of the new math. The classrooms were going along as usual while the nation's foreign affairs were going along less well. Thus, it was determined outside in that distant arena far from the School, called the seat of national government, that there was a shortage of math and science brains to carry us through the decades of the space age ahead, and the outside turned to look at the inside—the inside of those classrooms. Whether or not the classrooms looked back was unimportant (to everyone except the teachers perhaps) because the outside pressure decided that what was being taught in those classrooms was not good enough: they decided that crash programs had to be initiated to make an educational breakthrough which would produce the manpower needed. Teachers did not lead nor attempt to lead the way in changing the math curriculum: they did not control the events that were to follow, as they might have, by creating to fill the need. Even though they had not identified the need from the first, even though they had not been aware that what they were doing was inadequate, they could have emerged as directors of the process of the math revolution. Their training in the field, their professional abilities could have plotted the direction, could have communicated the issues to their colleagues. But no—the university professor of mathematics came down from his tower and brought the gospel of change. The practicing mathematician squeezed past the educational guardians and made his way out of the fields of the intellect where mathematics was a philosophy, a language, and an art into the wastelands where it had become but a required subject suffocated between the pages of yellowed outlines and mildewed textbooks. So it was then, uninvolved teachers saw crash training programs designed, small research groups formed by "outsiders," textbook companies dashing to the source of need where everyone ran to pick up the cash customer.

Teachers may or may not have known that the old math would not stand the light of the new day, but whatever they knew they were not involved enough in the changing scene that was their home base to be ahead of the changing math curricula. Reading, 'riting or 'rithmetic, we must not be caught like that again! *Teachers must see change as their responsibility.* For them there can be no basic morality in closing their minds to the real world of real people and real events. Teachers just have to know that the real world is filled with change and that they have to be prepared to deal with it. They have to understand it. They have to expand because of it.

How can teachers accept the responsibility of shaping the minds of the young if they do not see their own relationship to the changing order, the place of knowledge in this order, and the evolving nature of the order? Knowledge is no more static than are the tides. As the shore is washed by the tides, knowledge is washed by all the movements of the cycles that form the universe. Teachers cannot be responsible teachers or responsible citizens either unless they choose to accept the inevitability of Ovid's observation that "All things are in a state of flux, and everything is brought into being with a changing nature."

As the child before them changes, the ideas in the book he holds have changing applicability. Even as the applicability changes, new texts are being written, new presentations are being planned, new techniques of expression proposed. The teacher is responsible for putting all of this in perspective, responsible for dealing with it, responsible for contributing to it.

The teacher has a responsibility to accept change as an alternative, to use its dynamics and to become a leader through this use. The teacher has a responsibility to contribute to change. Apathy or neglect become ingredients of immorality.

The alternatives seem to be to wallow in the mire of fear and self-pity because change is threatening the safe little pigeonholes of our existence, or to see change as an opportunity that can lift us to fantastic heights of leadership at the peak of anticipation and can help us mold tomorrow's leaders.

The choice is ours to make now while there is still time. Soon, very soon, the choice will have been made and the need for those who resist change will be no more.

A CASE STUDY

Scene: Teachers' Lounge, Elementary School Building. Suburban district. Pay good. Working conditions just fine.

Actors: Principal and crew: twenty-one teachers. Eight have been in this same building for over thirty years; six have over twenty-five years in the school district; three have had upward of five years of experience before joining the staff here; two are first-year teachers; one has been transferred into the building because her principal had a nervous breakdown and she could not get along with the replacement; the remaining two had between five and ten years of teaching experience before their own families came along when they left teaching to which they have just returned. One of these was once the PTA president in this very school.

Subject: Teacher training for the new math program.

Principal: "Well girls, we've been told at headquarters that we're going to have a new math course of study, new textbooks—the whole thing. And they are bringing in a Dr. Bronstein from some Eastern school to train us in all the new theory. We'll meet every Wednesday afternoon from 3:30 to 4:30. School will be dismissed on those days at 3:00 to allow us time to get to Toneville Junior High where the meetings will be held. There will be no absences. The superintendent is very anxious to have this go and we are spending a lot of money on this together with the Toneville School Board and the Liberty School Board."

Miss Ellsworth (*an old-timer*): "Gracious, June (they have known each other since they were really girls), how much do they expect us to do? Is there no end to their demands? Next thing we know they'll want this sort of thing in all the subjects. I say we're starting something that we'll all rue."

Miss Hendricks (*another old-timer*): "I agree with that. It's a fine day when some college professor has to tell us what to do. Some of us have probably been at it since before he was in diapers. Now everyone's telling us."

Principal: "I don't think that's in back of anyone's mind. It's just that so many new ways of doing everything have come about that we have to keep up. They told us, someone from some research group—I forget the name of either the man or the group—but they were telling us at this meeting with the superintendent that since Sputnik we just don't have enough good mathematicians to keep the country going and it's all very dangerous. I even think the government is in on it. So we have little choice."

Mrs. Lucas (*the former PTA president*): "You are so right. Why Jimmie (her son, and his mother's favorite) was telling me that at college no one does math the way I did or do it. He says I'm not quite with it but that it's all right for the little kids because no one expects them to learn anything down in these grades anyway, but that when you get to the upper grades everything is different. I can't even make heads or tails out of his simplest assignments. I remember when I used to be able to help him—but no more. Seems like everything he learns is just Greek to me. If only Jim, Sr., were alive. I still think that the kids would be better students. You need a man around for that certain touch I think. I'm all for going to these meetings. They'll help me with Jim, Jr."

Miss Kerry (*the one whose former principal had the nervous breakdown*): "Well, I just don't know how I'll be able to manage. It takes me forty minutes to drive home and with the winter weather and all if I have to go to another meeting I'll get home so late it'll be time to turn around again to come back to work. As it is I'm exhausted having changed from third to fourth grade this year."

Mrs. Bernaby (another one with a family): "That's just the sort of thing that bothers me. I have a longish drive and you know how I have to pick up Mercy (her nineteen-year-old daughter) on my way home, and as it is she has to wait for me twenty minutes or so, and then I've started going to the doctor for allergy shots and those appointments are on Wednesdays. I don't know how I'd ever change the appointment."

Principal: "Now look, this is all out of my hands. I tried to tell the superintendent that there would be sacrifices and hardships involved in this but he never asked any of us principals. We weren't consulted. This is just the way it goes. We were told and now you'll have to cooperate. As it is I expect I'll have a lot of trouble with some parents who will want to know what's going on that we have to have an early dismissal on Wednesdays. I haven't figured out how all of that will work yet with getting the youngsters out of here and the bus schedules changed and all sorts of other complications I'm sure we haven't even thought about."

Miss Swanson (twenty-four years in the system): "Well, that's my point exactly. It's come to a pretty state when we're treated like so much baggage and not even asked our feelings. That would never have happened when Mr. Riley was here (the former superintendent who was with the schools for thirty-nine years and who discovered many of these girls when they were still in normal school and brought them along with him into the system. He retired last year). He thought about us as people and he would have asked our advice. We never would be told after a decision had been made and embarrassed in this way in front of the parents. And who gets the idea that we need new math anyway? It was good enough the way we've been doing it all these years. Why isn't it good enough for someone Sputniking around? Maybe we'd all be better off if we didn't have such things anyway."

Teachers (a chorus of mixed voices from a variety of types): "She's right. Leave it to Swansie to tell them off. She's not afraid and she's right. Can't we protest or something? We need to have a voice in what's going on."

Principal: "I know how you feel, girls, and I don't think there's a thing we can do. The Board of Ed. is behind this whole thing and I bet that Mr. Arnold (an assistant professor at a local college specializing in engineering and a critic of the schools because his son is gifted in science and he has not been challenged. Mr. Arnold thinks that the school is holding his son back and that the boy won't get into Yale because of it) has had a big voice in all of this. You know what trouble we've had with that family and the way they think they can run the schools."

Miss Seldom (*in the building for twenty-eight years*): "Well, let's demand a formal statement of what we've been charged with doing so wrong that we need to be trained during our free time. No one really knows what a teacher's life is like. I'd like to see the average person be able to put up with all we do: the papers, the children, the parents, and all the pressures and uncertainties."

Teachers (*two simultaneous echoes*): "Why don't they pay us for going to the meetings?"

Principal: "There has been some talk of that. I guess they consider they're giving us something because we have some release time for this since school is dismissed early and since legally I guess we're actually supposed to be in the building after school until four o'clock anyway. So all that they're taking is an extra half-hour. And I guess they're talking about applying some of this toward salary increment, but it hasn't been worked out."

Miss Dwinder (*one of the new ones*): "I'd like to volunteer to be the building representative to the Board if they decide to have a committee to look this whole problem over, what with the questions of getting paid, getting credit and having time off. I bet there'd be some hot arguments and I'd sure like to get in on it. They told us at school that if you wanted a career in education you had to get involved and I guess I've always been good at shooting off my mouth."

Principal: "That's fine, dear. If they ask for such a committee we'll take a vote on the representative."

Miss Ellsworth (*the first old-timer who spoke*): "Leave it to the young to come up with good ideas. I think we should press for such a committee and refuse to go along with these meetings until a committee has studied the problem in more detail. We can't rush into every new cock-and-bull idea that comes along."

Teachers (*lots of voices chirping in unison*): "Right. Exactly. Yes.

20

That's it. Sure. Exactly. Every new idea. Committee. Demand it. Right."

Mrs. Underwood (the other new teacher): "My husband tells me every night that what teachers need is a more active pressure group. This is what the Teacher's Union is good for. It's an active pressure group. We should use them in this whole matter."

Principal: "Now, dear, our building has gotten along without the Union which is really quite new in our system and as far as I know all of our teachers support our Teachers Organization which for over forty years has done so much for our system. And in our building we have had two presidents of the Teachers Organization and I once was Vice President."

Mrs. Lucas (the former PTA president): "I still have very good relations with the parents and still keep contact and quite active in the PTA and I'm certain that we could get mothers to help us. Lots of them come to me and tell me how they are really concerned that we have so much to do and have asked how they can help."

Miss Belle, the school secretary, interrupts the meeting. She leans over Miss Hendricks to whisper to the Principal.

Miss Hendricks: "Why, Joannie Belle, your hair looks wonderful. You've had it done. I hadn't noticed before. Oh I do like it."

Principal: "Excuse me, girls. I'll be right back. Telephone."

A lot of buzzing and chittering follows with occasional words breaking through like, "Joannie's hair." "Everyone does it nowadays." "Too blonde for school." "Youthful though." "Some of the sixth graders do it." "What do you expect with the mothers around here in their tight pants going to the supermarket?" "Times changing."

Principal (returning): "Well, girls, that was Miss Burns the principal over at Toneville Elementary. We've been friends for a long time. Her nephew is married to a distant cousin of mine. She tells me that her teachers are in the same sort of state we are and that she is going to talk to the principal's group tomorrow at Toneville and compare notes. I think I'll do the same. I'll get on the phone tonight and check with a couple of the girls."

Teachers (spontaneous approval from all sources, all sizes, shapes and ages): "Good!"

Principal: "Just sit tight and keep all of this under your hat. I'll get back to you tomorrow. Don't forget that Albert Avenue is blocked off due to that broken sewer so watch it going home. Your class registers are due in the office tomorrow. Miss Belle has to check them all over. It's a big job and some of you will insist on making mistakes in adding up the columns. We have that new adding machine in the office and you can use it but you'll have to check off the time you want it on the sheet on the wall. Too many traffic jams and we just have to know where it is."

Miss Swanson (this is Swansie whom the group thought was so right): "Well I haven't been able to use it yet. I've never been able to find it when I've gone into the office. Why does it have to leave? It'd be much better if it stayed on the counter and we could just dash in at some free time. As it is I just give up if I have to track it down like a hunter and who wants to pull it away from someone?"

Principal: "Well, girls, I'll have Miss Belle work out a system for the adding machine and she'll tell you about it individually. We do have to help her out with the registers and add them correctly. It makes quite a mess, you'd be surprised, when even two columns are wrong. That's all for now. Oh, Mrs. Underwood (the one with the husband and the business about pressure groups and the Union), could I see you for just a minute please? I have something to tell you."

Two days pass and on the morning of the third day the principal has had Miss Belle, the school secretary, place a mimeographed sheet in each teacher's mail box. It reads:

To: All Teachers.
From: H. June Hamp, Principal.
Re: Math Meetings.

The math meetings are going to be studied by the superintendent. They're postponed for now anyway. A committee is to be appointed representing the buildings. We'll meet next Monday at noon for our election of representative. Our nominees are: Miss Ellsworth and Miss Hendricks.

Good news department: Shower for Elaine Dwinder at my place, Saturday at 1:00. She's engaged! Shower for Gert Underwood at my place, same Saturday at 1:00. She's expecting! Details to follow.

Sit tight, girls, and keep everything under your hats.

ANALYSIS

The foregoing case study is based upon an actual series of events experienced by the author. In the name of human decency, locations and personages are disguised. Yet the case study points up a chain of responses that might be said to characterize teacher mentality in relation to change.

These responses begin with the role of the principal and the teachers' interaction with her. Notice that H. June Hamp acts like a mother hen holding court over her brood. When a male teacher moves into this scene he is seldom, if ever, cock of the walk. The pecking order neuters his sex and he too becomes one of the principal's brood. She is on a girls-will-be-girls level of operation except where she is threatened by such dangerous ideas as Mrs. Underwood's injection of the Union notion and Miss Dwinder's self-propelled notion about her qualifications to serve on the committee. In the main, however, Miss Hamp has things under control and is not without her resources including those of an informal underground over at the Toneville school. The principals cultivate a broad field of this sort whereby the weeds that grow in their own back yard may be eradicated by the pesticides used in another yard. Miss Hamp needs to assert herself as principal from time to time and does so by inventing new routines such as the adding machine ritual.

The teachers show that those who have been around long enough get to feel quite nested in with the system and deal with Miss Hamp as they would any girl friend. Those who are less experienced try to inject into the proceedings the glad tidings of comfort and joy they have taken with them out of their college classrooms. Before those college notes get implemented, however, many a book will be yellowed with age. The teachers do not demonstrate any real educational leadership. They appear to be the recipients of decisions that have been made around them, almost in spite of them. They do not show any dynamic educational convictions but rather, they base their arguments upon self-centered needs completely irrelevant to the issues. Such things as after-school appointments and a break in their own routine seem of greater concern than the larger argument. They did not themselves anticipate the change and act unaware that there is a changed need in mathematics, but they nevertheless become defensive and protective. Their themes become melodies of what they have always done, how good it all was way back then, and "Why do things have to be as they are? Where are the good old days of yore when teachers were left alone?" The college appears as an alien world to them, not identified as being in partnership. Thus, they do not see themselves as educators on a par but as creatures put upon by outsiders. They admit to their inadequacies in mathematics but appear not to care. After all, there are other grades coming up for their students where all deficiencies can be remedied. They operate in an emotional whirlpool and the waters are easily agitated. Anything more is just too much. After all, the requirements of the job are terribly, terribly difficult. Nobody knows the suffering they see.

The projected mathematics changes are not the only kind that annoy. All changes do. Even the change in the bus schedule would be very difficult and the new plan around the adding machine will take a formal system to insure its operation. There will be everything to help except a lock and key and a Brink's truck. But then, Miss Belle, the secretary, will be custodial and keep the thing moving along.

They evoke the memories of the past, the days of Riley the retired superintendent when men were men and the girls were loved and wanted and protected. Tradition is their sweet recollection of twilights of tenderness. Today is not tradition and so it cannot be good. It must be treated with suspicion. There are all kinds of people to watch out for and all kinds of places to put the blame. The parents like Mr. Arnold may be acting up, or right within their midst colleagues may do suspicious things like provoking sentiment for the Union.

And yet, in the presence of a teacher like Mrs. Underwood who is aware of the value of pressure, we see one kind of force for change that has come to be a part of today's style. Witness the effects of teacher strikes such as in New York City and the results of teachers' protests through their active union sanctions. There seems to be a growing energy focusing upon the use of labor tactics to bring about the kinds of internal changes teachers want. Also, witness the new look of a Miss Dwinder who volunteers and tries to push forward into a position for contributing to policy making. The administration did not involve the teachers nor, for that matter, the principals, but went ahead and made decisions about mathematics. Yet, did the teachers and principals evaluate what they were doing with mathematics in the light of the new technological need for mathematics and the new world events that contributed urgency to the problem? Was there time for involvement? It appears as though time must be taken for involvement if change is to be brought about. Without involvement the issues get confused, as in this principal's meeting, and because of the confusion progress is stopped.

Notice how teachers demand inducements if they are to change. Hence, they come around to the triad of salary increment, release time, and experience increment. Teachers show themselves to be human first and teachers next. They will do anything to protect their comfort in a situation. After all, they will even think of getting the parents involved in helping them forestall something which would in the long run be a help to the very children to whom they are committed. Notice how important the informal level of interaction is with teachers like Mrs. Lucas using the parents and her PTA contacts and Miss Hamp using her contact with other principals in other systems.

The teachers get all tied down to the small details of the small world that they choose to make theirs. So, the adding machine becomes just as important as the new math and details for resolving its dilemma take precedence. The minutiae become the major concerns of a life that shrivels into a web of insignificance rather than being challenged by the larger concerns of a larger world.

Out of all this some positive things do happen. Although the math training sessions are postponed, the pressure to have a committee of building representatives goes through. This is a change in the right direction. Whereas the teachers did not exert leadership to demand changes in math and did not organize study groups themselves, when pressed to change they united in defense of their rights and demanded representation. This is the way the administration should have proceeded in the first place. The issue should have been identified, supportive evidence should have been presented, then representatives appointed to study the problem and recommend directions for action. The teachers should have been asked to advise antecedent to the decision. But then you can see that change itself is thus slowed down and that the course is delayed by actions that are of less importance to the ultimate goal. But without those actions the goal itself will not be reached. Teachers do not move easily and are not above sabotaging anything that they do not perceive as comfortable to them.

2. Societal Forces and the School

Men live together in groups. They join together around common interests and become societies. They have their behavior influenced by external forces, forces which eventually control through their power. These forces grow out of societal living, and as they buffet and affect the men in the societies, they buffet and affect the places of teaching and learning that men have created.

If we are to understand change we need to understand the nature of these societal forces; and if we are teachers we need to learn how they act upon the School. They can shatter the status quo and cause a flight into fear of the unknown or they can come as signs that are known possibilities, even probabilities, and merely interrupt us until we get our bearings, if not today, tomorrow, for the earth is rotating and there will be that other dawn.

THE SCHOOL AND SOCIETY

School is part of the very essence of our society. We insist that our young go to school and we require certain standards for the way they learn and what they learn. We insist that certain people are able to teach our young and that this and that are what we want them to teach and this and that are how we want them to teach it. It all adds up to our feelings of possessiveness. The School is ours and everything and everyone in it belong to us. We pay the bills. We run the show. And our frame of reference is the way it was done when we were there ourselves—no matter how poor our memory.

This adds to the fact that although the School is a national notion, it is not implemented in any singular pattern. There are differences that make schools in one part of the country seem like foreign institutions to other parts. The School often looks as intelligent or as ignorant as the people supporting it. It looks as open or as prejudiced, as liberal or as conservative, as yesterday or as today as the people who propagate the children they eventually send to the School. In some places the School challenges, in others it dares not challenge, in others it is challenged. There is no one pattern.

Man is the only animal who has abrogated the responsibility of teaching his own children. Unlike the animal who teaches each brood the facts of life, man has agreed to let someone else do the job. That someone else is the teacher, but man stipulates that the teacher must be in a setting immediately recognizable as *School.*

He does not want these places to be detached from him. So he keeps in touch by electing Boards to serve his purposes and to keep his interests protected. And no one will be allowed to forget that these schools are serving the parents who built them. And with all of this, the teachers will be kept under control. They will not be paid too much. Their heads will not be allowed to get too big. They will be necessary but not too valuable. And whether they come or go, the School will remain and society will go on venerating it while condemning it, blaming it while extolling it. For the School is a moral place where the teachers must be virtuous people free of any sins that might show and hurt the young—and where God should not be mentioned. He is against the law now, but there are ways of getting around it provided our sensitivities are not touched. You see, the School is a sensitive place and the citizens are sensitive about the Schools. The teachers can take on some of the job of being a parent to our children but they have to go carefully. After all, perhaps they should teach the children about human reproduction but it better be kept more abstract than positive. Keep the references to reproduction limited, whenever possible, to how dogs and rabbits do it and deal with the human aspects obliquely. Maybe black and white charts are all right but pictures that are too explicit could get teachers into trouble stepping on toes. The School is a mirror of society's values, society's hypocrisies. It is a barometer that rises and falls according to the metabolism of the people being served. It is swept over by tides that come and go, and fads that come and go, and Boards of Education that come and go.

The School is for all—maybe not for all together with races and economic levels mixed, but there will be a school for everybody. Attendance is legislated, dropouts are condemned, standards are upheld according to the norms of middle-class white America. Society wants the School to teach and society wants its young to learn—even if all schools do not teach well and all children do not learn. For along with motherhood and the flag, the School represents to the majority that which once was, may not now be, but nonetheless will go on and on. "Teach the young to read if you can," society says, "teach them to write if you are able, to figure with numbers. Teach them other things that will turn them out as products we can call literate and intelligent." Here the instructions become colloquial. "We'll give you the money to do lots of other little things here and there that we don't have time to do," the suburban society says. "We want them to learn to get a job," the laboring society says. "Make them understand that when we have given them everything it is foolhardy to risk alienation by taking drugs and pursuing cheap thrills," the rich society says. "Don't make them too emancipated," society joins together to say. "We won't know them. We want them to go on preserving the things we have built up for them. Go on, School, teach our young, but watch out. These are dangerous times, you know."

THE SCHOOL AND CHANGE

Although change is a constant part of the universe, the School does not change as the result of any automatic process. To the contrary, the School often appears to have established its own systems of resistance against change, its own process of being in conflict with change, of being a hyphen in the natural phenomenon of change as if intending to remind nature itself that it can punctuate anything according to its own will, even in defiance of any and all immutables.

As a rule change occurs as new ideas become absorbed into the fiber of the old to such an extent that replacements are visible in techniques, attitudes, and objectives. Change is seen as time encroaches upon tradition and makes the latter appear more historic than relevant to the needs and demands of a contemporary society.

But the School is a conserving organization, conserving ideas tested by society and generally reluctant to push aside its conservatism for the untested. Thus there often occurs a time lag between when ideas are new and vital and when they become incorporated into the modus operandi of the School. And here the education profession is at fault. The School is victimized by a lack of rejuvenating efforts by educators because the School is the workshop of a profession desperately in need of interpreting whether or not it is a profession. The School is a workshop where there is no common language, no highly developed theories that relate to its activities, and no common scientific bases upon which to formulate directions. Hence, while the educational profession struggles for a definition of its terminology, its theories, its formulations, the School stands resistant to replacements in its techniques, its attitudes, and its objectives. "How can we accept what you cannot decide on?" Although society is knocking at its doors with significant change, the School, having no voice of authority to listen to, remains devoted to its history of moving slowly before absorbing foreign elements into its midst. Chances are when badgered the School will say that it is always pushed to change in so many diverse ways that it has no choice but to hold its ground—that if it incorporated everything that came along, the education of the young would be a hodgepodge. The badgered School would probably add that it has a mission to withstand pressures to change because those things which appear to be relevant today often cease to be so tomorrow, and the only things that remain of certain value are the traditions that have been tested over generations.

Considering the fact that there is a measure of truth in this, the miracle is that any changes are effected at all. Almost certainly as a result of each change that is effected one could record a data book of hurt feelings, a multitude of threatened individuals, and a time schedule more like the creeping of a tortoise than the running of a thoroughbred.

The School does not run. It is not comfortable running. It is suspicious of running. It is suspicious of runners. Their course has not been charted and could be a detour, and the School is not an adventurous organization. Like the sloth, it wants to know where it is at all times and where it is is probably pretty close to where it has been always. Or, the distance to where it is apt to go will be traveled with slow and cautious steps, calculated, sometimes imperceptible, with frequent pauses lapsing into prolonged rests, thus the movement fails to have an impact when the goal has been reached.

What is more, the School does not have to run. That it should morally is one way to look at it. That it should in order to do what is most needed, in order to lead, and in order to set the course for what is ahead, are issues to be sure. But no one is in a position to coerce the School into facing these issues, and there is no matter of fact about change as far as the School is concerned. Its life is not dependent upon changing. It is not involved in an economic competition where buyers can refuse to deal with one concern or product. There is no threat over its head that the number two dealer is creeping up in sales. There is no number two dealer. The School is the School after all. Some parents may move to other districts to get different kinds of educations for their children, but this is no threat to the School. It is a corporate organization in the unique position of having been created as a monopoly by society to do what society has mandated. And so in spite of any weakness, no one is going to put it out of business. It will go on having the young walk through its doors and it will go on turning them out "educated," and as long as reproduction takes place the business enterprise will continue.

As one superintendent of schools told me, "They'll bring out one new gimmick after another—machines, computers, the whole bit, and they'll never replace the teacher. Good, bad, or indifferent, no one will get rid of the teacher and their schools." Or, as an elementary school principal put it, "After all, teachers may not be as smart as machines, but they can prove to parents that they know and love little children. And no one will let the teacher and schools be jeopardized when they use that argument."

The large industry that is education and the multitudinous warehouses that purvey its supplies, the Schools of America, are not accustomed to looking at the challenges of change. They are not accustomed to seeing their role in an international world, not accustomed to looking at the possibilities of providing leadership through innovative practices. These educational despots have for too long relied upon perpetuating old values. They have allowed other agents within society to interpret change and have deferred acting upon such interpretations until official commentary has come in.

The Schools operate at a slow pace and they gear their teachers to operate at such a pace. Part of this comes from the bureaucratic rituals which reinforce the ball and chain mentalities to which many teachers fall prey. How can individuals subjected to the weight of nonsense requirements be expected to burst forth as creative and exciting powers? When contented to drone away at levels of mediocrity, how can we expect minds to soar to new vistas? A bird whose wings have been clipped ceases to know the joys of flying.

FORCES THAT CHALLENGE THE SCHOOL WITH CHANGE

The time has come, however, when the alternatives facing the School have narrowed. Whether or not to change is coming to be less and less within the province of the School. Forces so great are coming to overwhelm the School with such power that unless the School makes plans to absorb these forces and work with them, they will overtake and shape the course of events anyway.

Through the years the School administration has learned how to deal with the bleating annoyances of its Boards of Education. The School expects as standard procedure that the face of its Board will vary from time to time and so hardly recognizes its resulting adjustment as change. The selection of a new Superintendent of Schools by the Board now and again is as much to be expected as churlish students and pained parents. As I was told recently, by the president of one such Board, "There is a weird thing that happens in American education. We are supposed to run our schools, but we hire a man to do it for us and we supposedly advise. Well, if we don't like him and he goes too fast we get tough and he quits and goes off to another school system that has need for his type at that moment. And at that time we go looking for someone who will keep things smooth for us while we get some levies passed. Then when things get too dull, we congratulate the man on what a fine job he did and he gets a better job elsewhere where his kind is needed, and we go out and get a circuit rider who won't stay with us long but while he does he'll stir things up a bit."

A Board member in another district told me, "We're on the pitch of keeping things fiscally sound now and so the business man has the best chance to win a place on the Board. But when we get fed up with all that lingo about keeping things in the black and all, we'll get some bossy housewife on the Board, some frustrated teacher type and she'll shout a lot and we'll begin to look more like a Board of Education than a Board of Examiners." And somehow, whether Board of Education or Board of Examiners, the teachers adjust.

The School has learned to live with and deal with the pressures for change from all combinations of Boards of Education, and no doubt such experiences have been stored up for future reference. But such experiences and such source material are nothing compared to the forces that confront the School today—forces that are beyond the community-neighborhood level. These forces are more apt to be macrocosmic in nature and their effects may already be hitting the community at the very moment they inject the School with strange influences.

For the first time the School is being forced into the awareness that it is a part of a universe undergoing dynamic change and that for every little change anywhere in the world, a resulting jolt may be felt at home. There is no place to hide from the chain of events. There is sometimes the possibility of stalling it a bit here and there, but eventually the forces will catch up.

ONGOING PROCESSES AND EMERGENT PROCESSES

For insights into the kinds of social forces there are and how they originate, we need to accept the fact that there are two kinds of processes being activated in the world: the ongoing and the emergent. The ongoing processes are necessary for sustaining human affairs and result in the kinds of continuing realities we all are accustomed to facing. We wake and we are hungry and we need food; either we hunt for it or we buy it, but some of us must raise it and some must reap and some must sell. We know that we must have the money to buy and that we must work in order to shop and cook and eat. Life must go on and the ongoing processes are those which sustain it.

The emergent processes, by contrast, disrupt human affairs and result in the development of new and different realities we must learn to live with because we cannot escape them. For example, what of the pesticides that have proved harmful to the food they are supposed to protect and we are accustomed to eat? What of the scarcity this creates and the resultant increase in cost of food that is available? New products, pesticides, interrupted an ongoing process of food production by creating upon it another process, poisoned food, with other realities, food shortages and high prices. Yet, it is unlikely that we will return to pre-pesticide days. Rather, we will see the merging of the pre-pesticide days with the future-looking pesticide days when through continued research harmful effects will be controlled and more highly refined types of pesticides will be introduced. In this process many jobs will be made available (an ongoing process necessary for the sustaining of human affairs), and continuous research will buffet the buyer with the results of changing technology of pesticides—the latter yielding emergent processes. Ideally, these two kinds of processes should meld together so that one overlays the other and one becomes companion to the other. The former keeps life going, the latter acts upon what is, modifies it and, hopefully, leads to progress—certainly change.

SOCIAL FORCES ON THE WORLD STAGE

These change processes are not without their own influence, for they unfold against the background of the larger social forces that contribute to, take from, and cause them. This background is the world stage. On this stage the actors are all the global societies of the world, such as the American, the Russian, the British, the French, the Arab, the Israeli. They interact one with the other and in turn all interact with the world. Hence, a Nixon and a de Gaulle cannot interact one with the other without their respective societies being put into interaction as a result, and the world is set into interaction as a result of American and French societies' interaction. There has come to be then, an extraordinary network of communication, both formal and informal, seen and unseen, that is intensified by our scientific powers to bring people together as never before possible. The world stage is not isolated any longer from the enormous cast of characters scattered all over the globe and representing all people.

Moreover, in this remarkable age of change there are social forces shared by every society on the world scene. However, these forces do not always act in the same way upon the individual societies and their consequences may be shaped by the peculiar circumstances of the society—by geography, climate, unique histories, national purposes, and other such dimensions. Basically, however, the social forces participating on the world stage are of five major types: emerging nationalism; space discoveries and technology; war and armaments; overpopulation, including the factors of poverty and disease; and shifting value structures.

All over the world we are able to see nations emerging out of old and traditional forms into independence. This reality has become a fact of life for the United Nations and may be seen on every new map as one country after another, in all parts of the globe, declares its right to have a place in the decision-making process of the world. Such emerging nationalism comes to be in direct or indirect interaction with all the global societies, including our own, and all of our own affairs become interrelated with those of these new countries. For example, the creation of the state of Israel and its conflicts with the Arab nations affects us not only economically and politically but morally as well. So it is, then, that nothing happening anywhere happens in a vacuum. There are no vacuums. Everything has become an open flow of energy with revealed impulses circulating in a dynamic field of activity.

Each of the other major social forces bring similar interaction.

The world stage is impatient with man's efforts to control his environment, improve upon it, eradicate the age-old troubles, provide an abundance of easy-does-it devices, make room for leisure, make human drudgery obsolete, increase life, decrease death, install new organs for old. There is a frenetic race to be first in space and an unceasing search to make the known out of the unknown: make new metals, find new stars, see into the cavities of the heart, dispose of the unpurified, make use of the waste. And the more man does the more there is to do. He must take care of the decay in his cities, the stench in his air, the stink of his waterways. He has a pill for birth control for a world population that does not even know how to take a pill. He has cameras to record him cohabitate and yet he will not look at the records that show him how his lungs are poisoned with hydrocarbons. Whatever his paradoxes, he goes on and on pushing against society and exerting forces that change day after day. It is as if he were saying that through his technology he will force mankind to recognize that change will ever be forced upon him through the sciences he created.

With deadly and prophetic devastation, the nations are thrown into holocaust again and again through the force that is war and as a result they feel the need to stockpile armaments. Arms have become a way of life, and, as every child has the right to his milk we have come to believe that we, as nations, have our right to armaments. We build this right into our economies and, in our interaction patterns among societies, use the lure of arms or the bribe of arms or the blackmail of arms, the threat and the fury, the awe and the agony, to attain our ends. But war and armaments are real in our time, not just pawns, and they grow more fearful with each passing moment. They have become social forces that are as real as heaving monsters waiting to hear the words of Revelations come to pass before they and we will be able to hear no more.

And the nations were angry, and thy wrath is come, and the time of the dead, that they should be judged, and that thou shouldest give reward unto thy servants the prophets, and to the saints, and them that fear thy name, small and great; and shouldest destroy them which destroy the earth.

11:18

The horn of plenty is running out, the space to run is being filled with obstacles, the air to breathe is pulsating with soot. Man is spreading himself over the land like parasites that destroy the life upon which they feed. The world stage has become overpopulated and man, with his potential to control, has not used his intervention to create and sustain the good life and overwhelm the life of disease and poverty. As it has been before, so it is now: the global societies of the world are battered by the social forces of disease and hunger. Food is what many need, food is what many want. And for every mouth that wants, there exists one more reminder of man's failure, one more reminder that for all that has been changed by the work of his hand, millions still await more change. And though the changes man would make be hindered by the cracking open of the earth or the spewing of the volcano or the tidal sweeps of the ocean, he will continue in his relentless search to control, to seek, to study, and to make different.

And as man goes on about his plans, for each change that occurs, the world cast of actors experiences a shifting of values. How can these remain static as all else moves so quickly? Values shift and, in the moving clouds of their passing, leave behind depths of unseen atmosphere still in need of probing. The values shift and often leave a void to be given dimensions which must be put to the test of time and the scrutiny of experience. But even while untested, these shifting values are a powerful social force, and they leave no one untouched. They are the way we think about what we think; they are how we look at what we see, how we listen to what we hear and what we do not hear because we do not want to listen. They are tolerance and intolerance, conventions and the lack of them, new fashions in what we wear and in what we do. They are the old revisited and the new rejected. Values shift around existing institutions, around the sacred and the profane, and nothing is immune: religion, marriage, education, politics, the body, the mind, drugs, travel, gurus, gods, death, burial, birth, artificial insemination, planned parenthood. Nothing is left to imagine; the world of possibilities has become the dialogue of values.

Such are the social forces, and they wash over the world in storm waves against which no battening is secure. American shores, European shores: they sweep across land where there is no water and across waters where there is no land. They are the forces of our time, unleashed upon a course of no return. They change and they are changing and even as they are changing they will continue to change. Nothing is safe from the hurricane-like eye that seeks out its target and sends down its winds. Only history will be able to record how well we dealt with the challenge of change—how many friends of the strangers we made and how many uses of the unknown we discovered and how we managed to survive and in what condition. For the time, the upheaval is too immediate upon us to evaluate its impact clearly.

SOCIAL FORCES ON THE AMERICAN SCENE
As one set of forces strikes out on the world stage, on the American scene others are moving about causing equal unrest. Here the cast of characters known as the American society is involved with six major elements of social force: the political, the military, the economic, the scientific, the social, and the moral.

Political stimuli reach out with tentacles that squeeze painful responses from the citizens, frantic responses in frantic times. They are times of hideous doubts that eat into the national being leaving a hollow autopsy of unknown causes, effects, means, and ends. The nation is filled with political unrest and uncertainties that cause a tottering as balance shifts from concern with our internal welfare status to concern with our role as big father to the world, from guardian of the underdog to watchdog over our own civil disobedience. Our political arena has become a circus of parodies on half truths, satires on deadly truths, fears over spills, and applause over bitterly won battles. Our circus is filled with loud-mouthed parties, flamboyant personalities, and the atmosphere is permeated with thickening dissent until the senses begin to darken, straining against the shadows of broken images and illusive dreams. The performing rings are saturated with the odors of strife-torn cities, littered with the wreckage of human denials: the sawdust of pretense covers stark realities too wretched to be seen without camouflage.

Intertwined within all this are the drumbeats of military spendings, military warrings, military warnings, military inevitables. All lie across us like a shroud that cannot be lifted, and under it our bones lie breaking even as our muscles twitch for survival. Vietnam rings out like a cacophonous chord into nights of atomic foreboding. Stockpiling missiles, experiments with toys of destruction, firing into space, inventing powers to disembowel humanity: these have become a military diversion while a nation watches on late evening television to view the gory possibilities and the immediacy of it all. We have made of military commitment a way of life and to relinquish the commitment has come to be synonymous with giving up life.

Yet to support all of this, plus the internal struggle for dignity and rights and freedom from poverty, at a time when our national image is at its lowest ebb in the world, has become a matter of economic disaster. Faced with impending possibilities of fiscal chaos, we sit by and watch our taxes rise, our national expenditures escalate, our responsibilities internally and externally increase and know the state of balanced scales in our time to be an impossible dream. Money for the poor, the elderly, the impaired, the delinquent, the unwed, the addict; money for . . . for . . . for. . . . Our citizens have come to stretch out in an endless line of needs with endless hands awaiting coupons and certificates, licenses and vouchers. Even if no one says we should not, we have absorbed into our lives the problems of *how to*— how to give of plenty to others while supporting a life of plenty for ourselves. We have come to be an economically disturbed land pressured by political expediency and military necessities.

Giving urgency to all of our lives is the scientific hyperactivity of a nation of fixers and doers, inventors and modifiers, adjusters and reactors. We live in a day to day assault of science, in a never ending onslaught of awakenings, intimidations, interpretations, diagnoses, projections, prognostications. We have named science the god of our age, the road to our salvation, the answer to our safety, the keeper of our sanctity. We have become a land of laboratories, institutes, research centers, inquiry carrels. We search into, under, around, over, on top of, with, without. We compare, contrast, relate, analyze, specify, probe, and pound; and we leave nothing untouched whether human reproduction or planet sterility, space sensitivity or organic insensitivities. We have emerged as men in control over and in power of: we can create and we can destroy and we can alter and we can sustain. We have been born again in the image of science and as a result we have gained a lot and we have lost a lot, but gain or lose we cannot turn back; we have to go forward conquering more lest we be conquered. Conquer or be conquered has become our fear and we say we will not capitulate; science will lead the way.

The impetus of social forces is pushing us into varying degrees of ambivalence. Certain of our established relationships have undergone changing emphases, such as the conflicts between white and Negro races as the Negro asserts racial identity; such as the relations between the sexes, between adult and youth, parents and children, authority figures and constituencies, the church and its followers. In every facet of life relations have undergone direct or subtle redefinitions. Likewise, we have become more aware of social conditions relating to areas not formerly a matter for our concern. We now become engrossed in the pathologies of difference, in the emotionality over differences, in controversy, and in protest. We have made the suffering of the Negro, the American Indian, the Puerto Rican, the Appalachian white a matter of living-room conversation. We have brought the narcotics addict, the homosexual, the nymphomaniac, the frigid woman, the impotent male out of gutter talk and refined these subjects by giving them the look of sophisticated peeping into other people's bedrooms. But out of it we have developed a greater awareness of man as a social being, of his universal needs, his similarities, his variabilities. We have come to see that it is appropriate to be involved in all manifestations of the human condition and that we can, through enlightenment, help and not persecute, love and not condemn.

But socially we have grown pseudo as well. We have confused superficial reading and superficial discussion with insights; we have confused cursory knowledge with empathy. And a lot of what we have done has been to salve our consciences or to boast of our being so grown-up, so open, so "everything goes." In the meantime, we have yet to take the challenge that is ours and to use openness and candidness as a resource that can channel energies toward honest doing for others, honest acceptance, honest non-judgmental behavior.

We have seen the family weakened as a central force, the church lose its authoritarian magic, the restrictions of segregation lift, conventions undergo re-examination. And with it all we have seen people coming to care less for amulets and clichés than they do for self-expression. But much of the self-expression, for all of its social courage, lacks maturity and takes on the look of exploitation, self-aggrandizement, hedonism, and sensory convenience.

Socially, we are in the process of evolving new systems of interaction, new patterns of acceptance, new manipulations of human involvement. This is a state of flux we are experiencing, a period of moving out of one state into another, a state of knowing what we do not like or want but not knowing where we are going or how to get there, not knowing what we will have when all has been spent. We have lost control over our social plans, and our movement is as so much flotsam fluttering in the wind waiting to fall to earth into some kind of design that will be appealing and wanted. We are in limbo evolving, but we have not evolved.

This evolution is colored by contortions in the area of morality. We have become a land thrown into pubescent fantasies of sex and sexual minutiae. We exploit sex and are exploited by it. We have commercialized it, sold it; been commercialized and been sold. Our nation has come to be one large billboard advertising sex. The orgasm has left the private state and has become subject for movie, book, song, and dance. The land has turned into a convulsion of onanistic self-indulgence. Exposure to anything anatomical is available anywhere. The sex act in any form and in all forms may be seen anywhere, discussed everywhere: it has become a computer process with mechanical selectors for making pleasure sublime. Love is an old-fashioned need. The love that surrounds sex has come to be a bore, an emotional problem that gets in the way. Fun is the banner and it is waved with phallic splendor in pulsating rhythms and psychedelic beats.

We call it liberation. Youth is demanding it and exploring with it. The adult world is experiencing it. In many a social circle love thy neighbor has come to mean sleep with thy neighbor. Liberation means that we drink a lot of alcoholic beverages, that we escape down many interesting pathways like a wolf longing for his primordial state, moving with aching instinctual steps toward his painful cohabitation with nature. We are a wild lot with nothing to lose. We have seen it all and we know it all. We have lost the hymen and can be violated no more. We thrust forward with defiant penetration into forbidden areas and we tear off the garments and render everything naked. Nothing can be hidden. These are times of modern spirits: there is a way of dressing in the spirit, talking in the spirit, being with the spirit. One large current fad has become a part of our economic way of life with youth culture a dominant force and alienated youth a popular topic. Pre-marital sex is one's own business. How to make sex more enjoyable is the publisher's business. Public lovemaking is expected; not to is a social matter that alerts to public warning—a pervert in the making. To drink is to be human. Not to drink is to be nonconforming and even a hippie has to conform. A nation of parasites living off the fleshpots of sensual fulfillment is where we may be headed. A nation of sex-hungry adolescents playing with adult issues of life and death is how we probably appear. Are we no better or worse than any other nation now or ever? Are we just growing up, facing challenges to expose how silly emphases are when placed on the natural functions and needs of man? Are we learning perspective, giving ourselves the chance to sort out the real from the unreal, the important from the unimportant? If so we should get on with it. We are too long at it. There is too much moral tension because of it, too little sense of direction. If new conventions are emerging, let them emerge. They are too slow in being gestated. If we are moving away from using sex as the yardstick of virtue, let us get on with it.

Meanwhile, churches go about their business, homes go about theirs, and we all go about ours. It is like a masquerade with everyone aware of the fact that truth is disguised but afraid to reach the witching hour and reveal true identity. Is it that the identity would be too shallow, too unseemly to accept as our own? Is it that we do not want to face it collectively? Is it better when it belongs to the others over there, better when they are the statistics and we can sit back and frown over how dreadful it all is? Well, repression is not the stamp of today. More likely, the stamp is frustration over the unrepressed and over the lack of fruit this bears. Man never found himself by finding an orgasm. Woman never found herself by finding a new contraceptive. Finding oneself means the discovery of communion, of extending beyond oneself, of giving, of loving more than one is loved. A nation finds itself in the same way—through communion with all its people and all the people of the world, through extending beyond its own needs, through giving and not expecting to have returned, through loving.

Sad, but America tries to do this and yet it fails, fails to make people understand its intentions, fails to communicate to its own people what, why, and how it is doing. We pay for communication and we do not have it. Sad. Our moral fiber is raw because of it. We have been too abrasive with the feelings that really count. We have been arrogant. And yet we have tried to be good. Like a child, we are caught time and again doing that which is wrong, but we cannot admit it and we cannot seem to learn from it, and we punish our own. Yet we go on because, wonder of it all, we are America and as long as we remain so there will be hope. This we know and this makes us strong. We will not accept anything else. We dare not think of anything else. Like that child, we have our dreams and they may turn into nightmares, but we go on dreaming because in that harbor The Lady goes on holding the lamp of our liberty.

THE EFFECT UPON THE SCHOOL

One of the testaments of that liberty is the School which receives repercussions from all the foregoing elements. It receives the effects of our political unrest—national, state, and local. The School can become a political pawn and it reflects political whims and follies, strengths and weaknesses. The School is part of our way of life. Education is big business but it is also big investment in the future of the nation. Its direction is the responsibility of the local citizenry, but the influences of national political events are visible. Where is the taxpayer's money being spent, how, and on what scale of priorities? What things are valued in this nation of ours? What things are considered more necessary than others? How can we supply the needs of the world and our own? How can we pay for poverty and education, for Vietnam and education, for weapons and space, for missiles and planes and education?

Each of the elements of American society adds its tone to the School, its coloration, its sets of conditions, its formulations about problems, and ultimately its impact. No one can deny the impact of the economic element with its implications regarding spending, identification of priority areas for development, funding for special projects, urban renewal programs, support to education, building grants. The taxpayer is sensitive to the economic structure of America. He needs to plan for his own life within this structure and thus where his pocket-book is affected he, in turn, affects. He wants to know not only the general areas to which his money is allocated but also where within those areas it is going. He wants to know how the School uses his money, what it uses it for and why, and he asks whether or not he is getting his money's worth.

There is the impact of science. Its strength is felt through its contributions to the technology of education, to the content of the curriculum, and to styles of instruction such as the inquiry and problem-solving methods.

Surely there is also the impact of the highly visible interaction between the social changes in America and the values and expectations of the youth the teacher teaches. These are the moral concerns, commitments, and reactions of America and how they tend to shape the goals and purposes of education, adding new responsibilities such as sex education, traffic education, and drug education.

Young hands in primary grades take the blob of plasticene given them and begin to pull at it and push at it and punch at it, trying, however awkwardly or adeptly, to shape it. Their hands shape, but hands are not the shaper alone for they were themselves shaped by heredity and by environment. And the School is like that blob of plasticene. It is being shaped by many, many hands, by all of society; but that is not all. It is being shaped by the heredity of its traditional role and the expectations for that role, and by the environment that is America during a crisis period. It is being shaped by the environment in which the major elements of social force—the political, the military, the economic, the scientific, the social, and the moral—are constantly pulling it, pushing it, punching it; trying both awkwardly and firmly to shape it. The School has its heredity and its environment and the shaping process of these societal forces within its environment are what have to do with the School and the teacher.

THE EFFECT UPON THE TEACHER

No one expects the teacher to drop dead in despair over world conditions, but he certainly should know the conditions. They are shaping him just as they are shaping all other men in the global societies of the world, and consciously or unconsciously, he is responding to life in terms of the attitudes and reactions, the knowledge and the concerns he has developed toward the world and the processes that are a part of it. But if the teacher does not want to stretch his reach out beyond his present grasp, if he does not want to include in his scope the British or the French, the Arab or the Russian or the Israeli scenes, he still is not free to pull a curtain down between himself and the American scene. He is a part of American society. He acts upon it and it acts upon him. He lives in that reality. His life is directed by its elements. And just as these forces shape the School they can shape him into a meaningless rubber stamp image unless he takes and uses them, unless he stands up and gets counted as one who molds while being molded, one who shapes while being shaped. That shaping is teaching; it is also creativity. It is taking the existing material of the universe and working it into patterns of one's own design, making of it something that was not before.

That is what is so exciting about all this. It is not discouraging. It is not depressing. It is exciting, and nothing has ever been as exciting before. The teacher can use the elements to help shape minds that will go out into a world of easily accessible transportation, a world of lightning communication, a world no farther away in its remotest part than the opposite coastline of the United States once was to many of us. To be absolutely practical, although the teacher may not be able to see the total environmental change affecting the School and him, he cannot fail to see that the content of what he teaches is being shaped by those elements. New ideas are being introduced into subject matter as a result of scientific, military, and economic changes. New attitudes must be dealt with as social and moral elements change. New ways of doing things are being presented to the teacher. And he really has little choice because the students before him are already being shaped by these elements and they need the teacher. Their attitudes, their convictions, their confusions, their searchings, their reachings, their hopes, their needs: these are all there and they are there because the elements of social force have made it so.

At no time has the teacher been given a greater challenge. He can take these forces and bring them into focus for the student by providing a forum for analysis and evaluation. He can take the turmoil that exists all about and bring stability to it through the use of his training and skill. Because he knows the young and how they learn, he can allow an airing of the forces, the interactions, the processes, and can give students a scheme upon which to base their actions. The teacher can use the elements of social forces as his instrument, as his curriculum; and through his process of instruction he can activate minds and lead them to awareness and understanding, to the ability to evaluate and select alternatives, and to plan action leading to eventual solutions.

It is in this latter area that the teacher gains his immortality. Although one hopes there will be many, it comes when one student, just one, is able to leave the schools of our land and because of a teacher move out into the American scene, or wondrously onto the world stage, and bring about some change to the benefit of mankind. And how did the teacher cause it to begin? It might have been because of the teacher's painful probing into the forces that are the realities of living; because of his attempts to translate those forces into conscious resources in his own life and make them part of his strength and his mentality, and then to communicate them to young minds. In this communication there is no indoctrination, there is no apathy, there is no lethargy, there is no doom, there is no despair. In the communication there is honesty, reality, relevancy, and a courageous attempt to teach within the real environment that is the School in the world that is today. In that communication there is the hope that out of such teaching, minds shaped with greatness can emerge unfettered by hypocrisy and released to do and to give.

It is a challenge and a privilege that should make the teacher proud. He is part of an honored calling. He does not have to be apostolic, but he can be great. Even if it be just one freckle on the face of time, it is worth all the study, all the probing, all the self-evaluation that brought it about in the mind or minds that he helped shape.

3. Pressures upon the Teacher

The School is a way of talking about an aggregate of people who function moving toward common purposes. The School is a way of dealing with the problems of interaction when a given number of individuals respond to a mandate of society and in so doing cause events to which others have to respond. The School is a business, a ritual, but it is bare without teachers. Teachers are the School. They are the participants in the ritual and no matter how depersonalized that ritual, it will not be performed without the involvement of teachers. They are contained within the School, recipients of all the forces to which the School is subjected, all the forces to which society is subjected. They have the power to modify and to change the structure in which they work and live. They have the power to use the energies of the societal forces that batter against the walls of the School, but only as they come to an understanding of those forces, of what they are, of how they come about, of where they are going.

Teachers are the School but teachers are also persons. They are the receivers of the gifts all persons receive. They are the victims of the follies all persons face. They are a part of life and living, a part of being and becoming; and because they do not exist in a vacuum as some special organisms furloughed from the world, because they are so real, so vulnerable, they face the continual pressures that flood across all of life.

THE PRESSURE OF CRITICS

Society is a powerful external pressure upon the teacher. From all quarters of society the teacher is being asked and even told to change. The channel is in the voices and pens of the critics of the Schools and their teachers. These critics, a most interesting group themselves, come from every pigeonhole and crevice of life.

There are the non-professional critics of all sizes, shapes, and dispositions. Some of these use education as a soapbox to air their various frustrations and seldom forget that education is often good for sales. Then there are the more sincere non-professional critics whose involvement in education is often more emotional than informed. Still they have their right to freedom of speech and they exercise it. Whether or not they maraud the rooms of teachers or walk lightly in the corridors, their effect is usually one of stirring up a ruckus. They include the observers, the spectators, the commentators, the journalists, the threateners, the cajolers, the wives, the unweds, the about-to-be's, the speakers, the viewers, the readers, the letter writers, the bitchy ones, the apologetic ones, the ones who know how hard it is to teach but . . . , the ones who warn of impending doom, the laughable ones, the deadly ones—every imaginable kind whose number would take a slide rule to calculate. They all think they know about education and they all think they care about education and they all criticize education and their criticisms become massive pressures upon the teacher.

Then there are the professional critics. They bring more informed criticism, it would appear, but often they bring more nastiness as well. Perhaps because they bring more theory, more "I've been there myself" credentials, their probing fingers come closer to the quick. They may sprinkle their words with deep meaning and they may show that they do in fact have an involvement and they do in fact know what they are saying. If all do not, those who do leave their sting. Nor can they be sent on their way with a shrug of calloused shoulders, for the critics path forever follows the teacher's path.

Thus, the teacher is made to feel more and more aware that there is no way that is his alone, that all he does is public property, belongs to the conscience of society, and will be scrutinized by society. All he does will be viewed by those who are socially responsible as well as those who are irresponsible. But above all the teacher becomes aware that everyone sees it as his own right, yea often even duty, to criticize the Schools. Like a giant hand, society's critics write in unison with words that sear or with words that inspire, but they write. Like a giant eye, society's critics see in unison with multiple visions that burn or with visions that are too frightening to behold, but they see. And like a giant ear, society's critics hear all, hear before words are spoken and after words have been said. They forget nothing: they use sensory apparatus like probing rods to dig deeply into the viscera of the teacher. Like massive X-ray equipment the public critics of education leave the teacher no place to hide, nothing that can be hidden, no privacy, no secret places, no modesty, no recesses that are not open to view and once open due for evaluation. The teacher is the School and the teacher is public property and that property is part of America's conversation, constantly. Like a theme that is committed to innumerable variations, the teacher is a motif that accompanies "Of Thee I Sing."

There is no switch to flick off the theme for a teacher's ear that has grown weary of the tune. The critics, whether they come from universities or from kitchens, whether army generals or labor union chiefs, whether senator or senior citizen, coalesce into one voluminous voice echoing into every corner of the land. They make America ever conscious of the teacher and they make the teacher ever conscious that he is on view, that he is being seen, being observed, that he is ever onstage.

Although the teacher knows that because society wants and needs it, the school in which he operates will not close down, the critic makes the teacher aware that the same society dimensionalizes that school in terms of its human forms and those forms are the teachers. Society may not grasp the meaning of the total ritual that is the School, but it can latch onto the participants in that ritual and to those participants society plays the role of acolyte. Through the teacher, society "serves" the School. It finds its service as it intervenes in the life of the teacher, interrupts the teacher, interprets the teacher, involves the teacher, indicts the teacher. As it incites, indulges, infects, inflames, inflicts, influences, informs, infringes, ingratiates, inhibits, instructs, and invokes, society "serves" its School. The teacher is the contact, the one in focus, the one in the spotlight, and he feels all of this as a pressure to be faced, a pressure that looms high above his goals. For it is not a pressure in the abstract but one that becomes personalized within the various individuals who sit on the Board of Education. They represent all parents, and whether or not the teacher is aware of the way in which he is directly affected by the external force that is the societal critic, he is aware of the fact that the Board of Education is influenced by those critics. When the matter deals with ways of saving money, ways of protecting children, ways of getting something more for the child for the money being spent, the Board is alert to the critic and the critic becomes a real part of the School.

THE PRESSURE OF THE BOARD OF EDUCATION

The child who sees his mother hide away the Easter eggs until that special Sunday morning is not going to risk not getting them by fooling around unless he feels his fooling around will not matter one way or the other. The child who sees his father slip the quarter out of his pocket in readiness to be placed under his pillow on the night a certain tooth falls out is going to be absolutely certain the tooth does come out.

Well, the Board of Education is mother and father to the teacher. It has the money tucked away for those special days called salary time and few teachers want to risk not getting those eggs by displeasing the Board. It waits for the teachers to grow and when it is apparent they have, salary increments are the reward for career experience, for in-service training credits, and for college credits. Although it may be like pulling teeth for some teachers to manage earning those credits, they know that the Board is there waiting to reward them and so they pull to get the reward. Like parents, the Board can get irritated and angered by having so many things to do that each detail completed merely brings more uncompleted ones to light. Teachers are afraid that they might become one of those details. And teachers would prefer to remain anonymous to the Board of Education unless they can be reasonably certain that their identity is something to bring joy rather than irritation to its collective heart. The Board of Education is like a father who is expected to give punishment. And if the Board of Education does not threaten and punish every once in a while how can it maintain its image of power, of authority, of sanction? Its image depends upon its communicating to teachers that it can muster its strength in a real display of power every once in a while, and teachers fear that they might become part of that every once in a while. Teachers know that punishment by the Board of Education can come through salary strings that get pulled one way or the other, through programmatic changes that respond to public criticism, and through numerous other subtle and not so subtle management matters. The Board of Education is not to be feared as much during happy money times when levies are being passed by a contented public as it is during those times when money gets tighter and the Board's potency is dependent upon its use of fiscal grubbing and paring tactics. Naturally the teacher fears such times of collective testing.

The Board of Education has to approve the teacher's hiring. The Board of Education has to approve the teacher's tenure. The Board of Education has to approve any and all matters that deal with the teacher's promotion, and the Board of Education has to approve the teacher's salary and any change in it. It has to review any matters that could lead to firing a teacher. It has the teacher's life before it in a file that tells everything except the date of confirmation and distinguishing birthmarks. Perhaps some places require this information as well. The Board of Education has the ear of the community and hears its complaints. The Board of Education is *for* the community—of the people, by the people, for the people. The Board of Education is like bacteria. It is all over, everywhere, a part of everything and of everyone. The Board of Education has to approve changes in curriculum, changes in materials, changes in programs, changes in policy. It advises on all matters. It has to know everything, has to see everything.

Even when uninformed, it will tell you that it is informed or else blame anything it gets wrong on someone else's not keeping it informed. It is a good and a brave institution unto itself. The Board of Education has all these same powers over the Superintendent of Schools as well. He is their man and they are his hands and his eyes and his tentacles, his everything. The Board of Education is a part of the American way of life and a part of the way Americans want to run their schools. It can be a good instrument. It can be a dangerous one. It can be ineffective or effective. It is necessary like perspiration is necessary, like oxygen is necessary, like elimination is necessary, like sunlight is necessary. There is no other way. The other ways are worse ways. The Board of Education is powerful and teachers know it. They know it is like the rock. They know it can be strong. They know it can be capricious. They know its bastard side, its magnanimous side. They know that the Board of Education is a pressure. It is the bible in the family, the electricity under the tea kettle, the oath of allegiance. But, more, perhaps, it is like someone's old Aunt Gert who is quick to anger, slow to show any humor, unpredictable, rarely affectionate, best left alone and unfortunately something to be put up with till death do us part.

The Board of Education is part of the job and it can make the job pleasant or it can make it hell. Mostly, it acts behind the scenes and for most teachers that is exactly where they like the action. Few teachers go out to Board of Education meetings and few are highly informed about Board practices and politics. Teachers like to remain on their side of events and like the Board to stay on its. Only when something boils over or is forced to the surface do teachers get in on it. In the main, they operate aware that the Board pressure is there and they go about their way hoping for things to maintain themselves. Their teacher organization representatives can keep them informed. For them, the average teachers, there is just too much to do and they like status quo. Little ripples make for a large disturbance and too many ripples could be just too upsetting. So, while their Board of Education investigates some new salary scale or some new possibility in sex instruction, they want to go about their business pretending that the roof will never fall in on them. Only now are we beginning to see examples of pressure being exerted from the teachers' end of things through union activities in such mass demonstrations as make good news copy.

Today there are those who are beginning to say that teacher complacency has been a dangerous impediment to improving their working conditions. But essentially, for most teachers, theirs is a complacent life in a complacent shell and they ask that neither be shaken too much.

THE PRESSURE TO MAINTAIN A "TEACHER IMAGE"

With every national magazine and most newspapers featuring stories about education daily, weekly, and monthly, there is so much exposure to the varieties of views about teaching and the teacher that no teacher would be sane who did not recognize that his professional world is not his private world and that his would-be private world is also a part of his public world. It comes as no surprise that the type and style of life the teacher leads is a matter for concern to others and this does result in pressures upon him.

It is not as much of a problem for those within the conforming patterns as for those outside them. For example, it is perfectly all right to be an unmarried female schoolteacher as long as one fits the conforming pattern of the spinster type who does not care for men, who manages not to look at pornography much less pose for it, who can balance seeming obliviousness to masculine urges with the ability to tell little boys how to use urinals. The unmarried female teacher is generally expected to be a virginal type, sexless amoeba who decided to make other people's little children her life, using her bed for sleep and not for play. If the world wonders whether or not she ever had the experience of such play, whether or not she ever knew fulfillment and decides she must have, since she is such a warm, feminine woman, then it is best discovered that the experience is mixed with its sorrow, like the loss of a love in the war just before the walk down the aisle. On the other hand, if the unmarried female teacher is too young and too attractive she needs to be careful. She will do well to appear to be serious toward one fellow, probably one she can not marry until he has finished school at which time she will help put him through medical school. This will serve better than for her to be just looking around. She needs to avoid the impression that she dates too much and that she is too physical when she does date. She needs to avoid wearing clothes that are too seductive because teachers are supposed to be restrained and are expected to project the portrait of one who is more involved with books than with glands. If the unmarried female teacher was once married it is so much better if the lack of husband is due to death rather than divorce. If divorced, she would do well to let it be known that she tried to save the marriage, that the spouse was absolutely vicious, and that she suffered with so much valor and so much dignity that were it not so long in coming she could be nominated for sainthood.

The female teacher should be all woman but not too much woman, giving but not being given unless under conventional circumstances. She should be warm but never hot. She should be loving but loved only under conventional circumstances. She should be well dressed and never too undressed, soft of tongue but not too soft of limb, polite, practical, and preferably not too plump.

For the male teacher there are image problems as well. Since men are supposed to be men he should have the right to have sex but he had better be discreet about it. Far better that his premarital encounters have the look of the marriage search and that his dates be the comfortable non-flamboyant type, girls of good reputation who do not look bed-oriented. If married the male teacher would do well to get some children into the act as soon as possible so everyone will be able to attest to his happy married state. If no children do come along, it might be a good idea to adopt some to show what a pillar of the community he is, what good values he demonstrates. If not married, and unable to project the man-searching-for-a-mate image, the male teacher would do well to assume as sexless an image as possible, the psychological eunuch demeanor wherein all of his energies go into teaching and so none are left over for hanky-panky. He should appear as though he is healthy with sex but not too much craving it. It should appear that although he has had experiences, he has accepted the responsibility of controlling new ones forever more. No sensual adventurer he. Not one for too much sex, but just enough. He should inspire students to look beyond his own needs and functions and not to arouse any curiosities.

He would do well to be just as predictable, tidy, and cautious about many other things: about where he goes; about what and how much he drinks; about what he says; about what clothing he wears, not too faddish and not too expensive.

In short, teachers should be as close to superhuman as possible, relieved of as many human foibles as is believable. And you know, it is a wonderful teacher who is able to be all of that and teach too. They are the ones who can live beyond reproach, who can be extensions beyond the obvious and soar into majesties of deed and word. But not all are so inclined or so qualified, and those who are not will feel the pressures of subjective judgment concerning their actions, their styles, their rights, their tolerances, their denials. Although it is coming to be a trend in some places to be more concerned about the performance of the teacher than about his personal affairs, civil liberty being what it is, the expectation that the teacher be a "safe person" is still very much prevalent, however humorously one may treat the image required. It is still a preferred condition when teachers are able to impress parents with the image of their being safe, exempted from physical needs, super beings who live off the air, who do not form waste and dispose only of knowledge and humor, smiles and sweetness, sunlight's creatures who exude goodness, asking for nothing but to love children and to be given large classrooms with a desk for every child.

THE PRESSURE OF PARENTS

These parents, the parents of the children, are the necessary evil in the ointment. Without them there would be no reason to teach and with them to teach is often to groan under their weight. Nothing is too good for them because nothing is too good for their children. They form into parent groups to keep all their fingers right in the school pie. They organize annual events that keep them posted while doing "something" for the school: bake sales with soggy baked goods, potluck dinners guaranteed to put weight on the pot, paper sales that soak up the pouring rain which usually accompanies the event, art shows for the arty, flower shows for the flowery, no shows for the no show. With large attendance or with small they carry on. They are a valiant troop who are an institutionalized pressure around the neck of the teacher. But at least they are crystallized into a concept that can be given a name.

Not so with many others for whom there is no name that can be called, and if there were it might not always be polite. There are the parents who crawl out of the woodwork the moment junior cries because the teacher won't let him play the king in the class play. There are the parents who, the moment after the D grade has been given, flounce into the classroom with the testimonial about how wonderful Susan is, what a brave and noble little child she is: why, oh why does the teacher treat her so badly? There are the parents who protest because the teacher goes too slow, who protest because the teacher goes too fast. There are the parents who think they own the teacher, who think they own the school, who do, in fact, own most everything they touch. There are smart, smart parents who know they could do as well as the teacher. There are the parents who know all about the teacher from all the parents of all the children who have ever had the teacher. And those parents, all those parents of whom there are so very many, are a pressure—an ever present, grinding, relentless pressure.

There is Mrs. Honeybaum who ran to the principal to complain. There is Mrs. Stephens who has taken the teacher into her confidence to tell her that Mr. Stephens is impotent and that is why Hildie has problems with arithmetic. There is Mrs. Dowderphine who takes William out of school because he cannot stand the teacher and gets William moved to another teacher. There are the parents who treat the teacher as a servant, those who patronize the teacher with trying to treat him like a social equal. There are those who coo because the teacher is such a dedicated person: poor soul, he could be making more money elsewhere, wonder why he went into teaching? There are those who try to make friends, and those who gossip to the teacher, and those who try the buddy-buddy approach hoping that buddies will give buddies' children good grades.

Oh yes, the parents. All those lovely parents. The remarkable thing is not just that this carnival of intervention does exert remarkable influence, but also why it does. Those parents who intervene are seen to be interested and in varying degrees their involvement is equated, by the School, with their interest and the amount of time and money they are willing to spend on the education of their children. Conversely, those parents who do not intervene are seen as alienated from the School, although this is not always true, and attempts have to be made to get them involved. They too exert influence and are a pressure upon the teacher, but the pressure is for different reasons and of a different type. Their children are often victims of their lack of concern and the teacher is often expected to be both parents and home. In playing this role the teacher is a source of anxiety beyond that of schooling upon parentally neglected children; and all the problems and all the deficiencies of these children, in turn, are pressures upon the teacher.

But in general the disinterested parent is in the minority. The average parent is interested in his child's education and that interest is shown in whatever way the individual personalities of the parents dictate. Whatever the way, it is a pressure. There are the pressures for the teacher to do what he is doing better; for the teacher to continue learning and growing; for the teacher to use new things, new materials, new techniques; for the teacher to be successful in making all children successful. There are the pressures for the teacher to be all things to all people, to be liked, to be able, to be faithful, to be top quality, to be a good bargain for money spent. The teacher is the commodity that has been bought and the parent retains the right to exercise influence over that purchase. The sale is never completed, never fully transacted, unless the teacher is fired; and while that unlimited warranty is in effect, the parent remains a part of the deal. Like it or not, that is reality.

The teacher is important to the child whose life is actualized around those experiences he shares with the teacher. His today is known only in terms of his yesterday. His expectations of tomorrow are based upon the events of today. Interestingly, many an adult lives in this same pattern with his only awareness of the moment based upon what came before it and his only vision of what is to follow based upon his life up to that moment. Whatever the metaphysics of the adult, if he is a parent he has to be in touch with the world that is important to his child and among the most important aspects of that world will be the teacher. As one parent said to me once when I was teaching the sixth grade, "My husband and I get sick and tired of hearing your name at the dinner table. It is always that you said this or you said that. And no one can disagree with you. You are The Word. We have declared you off limits in the house." While this was all said in jest (at least I've chosen to think so during these many years), there is a moral within the facetiousness. Parents are aware of the influence the teacher has over the priceless quantity that is their child's brain, and they must and should know all they can about so overwhelming an influence. Sometimes parents overplay this role, but for their many faults in doing what they do, they usually try harder to help than to hinder. They cannot remove themselves from the picture, and the teacher, no matter how sensitive he is to their good intentions, has to deal with the pressure of their presence.

Ironically, parents have a way of disappearing just when they are most needed. Let something come up that really requires their help and they always seem to be out shopping, at the hairdressers, at the dentist, somewhere else than available. Among parents, fathers are insidiously much more difficult to get. The taxpayer father, paying for the bills of the School, usually leaves the job of insuring his investment up to his major stockholder, his wife. Fathers are seldom available to teachers and are usually dragged to school only when it is necessary to defend their wives or to support their wives' positions, which often means fanning flames of already overheated emotions.

THE PRESSURE OF STUDENTS

Whether or not there were parents, whether or not their roles were taken over by automated propagation with needles and sponges, if children were the outcome, children would be the major pressure upon the teacher, and as long as there are children they will remain the single most potent external pressure upon the teacher.

These children are the students and when they become students they retain the needs they have as individuals and these very needs cause pressures. There are the physical needs, the emotional needs, the mental needs. Each entails, on the teacher's part, the providing of outlets for expression and sources of development, and the understanding of what is being done and why. As if this were not enough, in the process the teacher is confronted with myriad pressures that arise when one individual interacts with another. There are the annoyances of enforcing a routine, the tempers, the irritations. There are the regulations imposed upon the teacher that in turn must be imposed upon the students and the monitoring of them: when does the student arrive, when does he leave, where is he at this time, where is he at that time, how does he go to the lavatory, how does he move through the hallways, how does he sit in the auditorium, how does he eat his lunch, how does he do this, do that, come from where, go there. All kinds of details like these put the student under pressure and put the teacher under pressure to supervise both the patterns of flow and the confusion that often results. And while the student is being regulated in such a manner, so is the teacher. When does he arrive; where does he go first, second, and third; what messages has he read; when does he eat; what duties does he have; what emergencies have arisen; what situations need attention. Details, details that pound against the brain and make the job of teaching one part intellectual, one part mechanical, and one part the part that tries to keep the rest above the water line. Then there are the pressures of motivating the students, of getting their brains porous enough to begin soaking in the matter that will have to be squeezed back out at test time. There are the pressures caused by those who don't get it, those who get it but slowly, those who get it too quickly for the rest, and those who couldn't care less about getting it or anything else.

The job of maintaining the environment in which the student is to learn causes pressures and the job of providing the substance of what to learn causes more pressures. But these pressures prove in the long haul to be just one component. The larger one, perhaps the most intense one, is that which comes to the teacher from the student himself in terms of his demand for education. Whereas this may not be as visible in the elementary grades, by the time the student reaches the secondary school, the pressures to get an education have become fierce ones. Education has become the passport. Students know it. They know it when they fail to get enough education or the right kind of education. They know it when the draft breathes down their necks and they clutch onto education like a life jacket. They know it when they look at the ghetto, when they look into the jungles of underdeveloped lands, or when they see a rocket launched into space.

Students pressure teachers when they sit before them in need of that which they are not able to absorb, when they are so below standard or so without readiness, crying out in their needs against the scars of being unfulfilled. Students pressure teachers as they sit before them in need of the tools for college, in need of the equipment that will fulfill their dreams of medicine, of law, of biology. And they make their brains vulnerable to the attack of ideas, the unrelenting demands of effort and work.

Students do not create these pressures out of their whims or their fantasies of sadism. No, society directs the pressure toward them and they in turn direct it toward the teacher. The School fails them if it does not make them self-sufficient, if it does not prepare them to meet the needs of the adult world, if it does not prepare them to choose wisely from the many alternatives of good and evil and lead them toward success in terms of economic independence and spiritual security. The pressures are set as the colleges demand greater perceptions, greater insights, more knowledge. The pressures are set as industry demands greater breadth, greater preparation, more skills. The pressures are set as the world shouts out to the School that it needs human resources with maximum sensitivities in order to service the needs of its military arenas, its changing economies, its mobile growth patterns, its nation-building functions. The world needs citizens able to face, direct, and cope with challenge. A world without such citizens looks to the School as being responsible for some of the blame and the School turns to the teacher. He stands as the whipping boy of the world's conscience, and that is the epitomy of external pressure.

RESPONSE

How does the teacher react, how does he respond, how does he use the pressures that are like waves that swell and recede, recede and swell over him? How does his inner being shield itself from drowning in fear and recapitulation and self-pity? How does his inner being gird itself for the swim against the undertow of mediocrity and trivia and red tape as the waves of pressure surge against his ego leaving in their recessions exposed frustrations and misty successes? How, indeed, is the measure of that teacher and of that teacher's success toward not survival alone, but triumph.

There are two survival kits and they might be labeled "material motivation" and "altruistic motivation." Certainly anyone with the slightest fondness for the pursuit of truth would have the teacher idealistically motivated by the pressures that pursue him. But life cases are seldom so cut and dried that they can be labeled all positive or all negative, and often the seemingly totally material motivation is a quinine-coated chocolate. Such material and selfish motivation as professional advancement which is translated into the terms of salary increment, new positions, different titles, more visible prestige, can often become instrumental in leading to the individual growth of the teacher and greater worth to the students and the profession. More than one teacher, pursued by pressures that coagulated into a desire to get ahead and either get beyond the pressures, get control of the pressures, or at least get paid more for enduring them, have ended up more worthy teachers and better individuals. I was once told by a good elementary teacher who eventually became an excellent high school teacher:

"I love what I am doing. There's nothing that can beat working with fourth graders. But I've got to get out of here. I have to get back to school and finish my degree and get certified for secondary school. No one wants an old man in an elementary school unless he's a principal. And I don't want to be a principal. So I guess if I'm to go on teaching kids it'll have to be an older age group. I guess parents wonder why a man sticks with the little ones if he has anything going for him. Why doesn't he go out into the world where there's money to be earned? Does he hang on because he's some kind of pervert? No, there's just too much threat facing that kind of thing. I'm getting too close to forty to stay in the grades."

And from another teacher:

"I felt all right until I hit my late thirties. Then I guess I sort of gave up and had to face the fact that I was just another old maid schoolteacher. After a long while of depression I went back to school to get trained as a school psychologist. At least with some special skills I could manage to hide behind the look of one devoted to career and it wasn't so obvious, at least I hope not, that underneath it all was that single gal who didn't quite make it to the altar."

Or there was the teacher who told me:

"It wasn't my idea to go on to school to get the Masters. Who needed all that work at my age? One fine day the boss came to me and told me that I'd better get back to school to refresh myself in conversational French. He said that a lot of new stuff had come out and that he'd like me to be prepared to use the language lab before it got installed. So, next thing I knew I was accumulating so many credits that

I just stuck with it and finished the degree. Good grief, the money I spent will take me years to get back, even with the increment I get for having the degree."

Then there was the teacher who confided in me:

"Well, the kids left home and I got bored hanging around. I've always liked school so I thought I'd just go back and take course work and before I knew it I got caught and just kept right on until I got my administrative certificate. Now here I am getting ready to take over as an assistant principal!"

And I could not forget the teacher who told me:

"It was just too good a deal to turn down. I got paid and my wife and kids got paid to come along too, that's what it amounted to. It was like a vacation for us all while I was taking advantage of the NDEA fellowship. Pretty good deal, and when I got back they put me in charge of a special teacher training program in the use of audio-visual materials so I made some more cash out of the deal."

In spite of the motivation, none of the results of such examples can be deprecated. Whatever the original motives, the fact remains that as teachers go on to get more education, as they participate in institutes, as they continue in their pursuit of degrees, fellowships, and the like, they open themselves to the possibility of changing. Whether their initial intention is idealistic or whether it is dollars and cents, the act of being exposed to new ideas, new techniques, new personalities, can lead to an inward stimulation, can create a dynamic for an exploration of the unknown. When the teacher continues to pursue professional advancement, whether because of long-range vision or because of immediate needs and pressures, there is the opening up of a creative process. At the very least the individual makes himself available to be reached. He is not out of sight, away from where things are happening; he puts himself in line with the traffic of change and even if only through collision, he can become a part of change. Once exposed to the new, his own creativity can catapult him forward. Such a potentiality is the promise of greater movement toward change and away from a condition of inactivity with its qualities of apathy and lethargy.

Under the duress of needing more money, wanting a different degree, trying out for a new job, a teacher is apt to change a lot more than if he felt none of those compulsions and was satisfied to roam the pastures undaunted by goals other than those of being left alone to ruminate on the kernels of yesterday's harvest. The profession may make it too easy to withdraw to already cleared fields by not exciting teachers to find a pioneer spirit in the pursuit of innovation. Thus, initiative to change becomes impotent in confronting the question of why change, whether through material motivation or altruistic motivation.

What of altruistic motivation? Where does it begin? It begins with the innermost act, with the act of conscience, and becomes itself the pressure that is the most lacerating, the most revealing, the most capable of hurting and of satisfying because it is the most intimate. In the dark moments of the night when the stillness of shadows covers the threat of exposure, when the sounds of the day become far away echoes, the teacher is left to the truth of introspection. He is not on a stage before students and patrons, there is no role to play, no performance to give. There is only the moment suspended in the night, when the teacher can assess the rewards and the failures of the spent day. This self-imposed analysis becomes the pressure of morality, the honesty of soul-searching. It becomes the need for truth with oneself.

"Why change?" becomes an internal question that clings to the marrow of the teacher and forces him to use its answer as a pressure that motivates him to change. He has to look at himself and see his own need for change. He has to look at his students and see his need to change for them. He has to look at his school and realize that it will change only as teachers like himself are ready to help it change. He has to look at society and perceive that it needs his change. He has to know that his world has changed and that he must become aware of that world and ready to give to it, not as he has done always but as it needs his energies now.

When a teacher goes before a class of students he must be an ethical person. He must exemplify those values he would hope to communicate. He cannot turn morality on and off. His whole being must be a synthesis of what he knows, what he believes, what he expects, what he represents. He cannot go before the young and be ethical unless he is an open system available to receive the signals of change and able to respond positively to their cues. These responses convert themselves into the communication of changing and changed content, and into changing and changed means of using oneself as an intermediary between such content and the learner. Unless the teacher remains an explorer in the world of change—observing, questioning, learning, probing—he becomes a closed system. He becomes part of a ritual, a mask. He ceases to know how to relate to the world that is the here-and-now and becomes a fossil encapsulated within the fragments of what was once. The teacher has to be able to provide an environment that is filled with windows looking out onto the elements of change, to bring to light the mysteries and the insecurities of change. He cannot afford to provide an environment that is stifled in the mustiness of decaying papers, yellowed posters, cluttered closets, and functionless functions.

Through his internal being the teacher has to link himself to today's world. He has to become capable of assessing its formulations in terms of what is known about yesterday and has to be courageous enough to prognosticate about tomorrow through computations based on probability and variance, deviation and norms.

Above all the teacher has to become his own relentless critic. He has to drive himself to seek out interpretations of the new, has to force himself to face the issues that pervade a world evolving new modes, new conventions, new institutions, new wars, new fears, new inevitabilities.

He has to face within himself the reality that his future depends upon his ability to control the threats to man's security and that the future of the young depends upon the answers he and others like him will find. He has to see his role so clearly that the result is a self-directed mandate to face the dawn with a commitment to face change and to provide others with the skills and insights necessary for them to change. His internal voice should call out to him again and again, "Change yourself. Change yourself, and then you will be able to lead others to change." His prayer will become an evocation of change. His prayer will commit his energies to change. He will become an agent of change. He will be one able to use himself to pressure himself into the process of changing. Then he will be able to say as one teacher did to me:

> "One fine day I stood before my class and I realized that I just didn't know enough to answer them correctly. They were much more with it than I. Even their questions were more intelligent than my answers

would have been. I felt like a cheat. I knew that something had to happen and so I started cramming and getting in the swing of things. Finally I brought in a pile of new books and a bunch of filmstrips and I began to learn on the job, I guess you'd say. But even if it wasn't the best way of doing it because those kids got a rotten break, at least I was able to give the next ones more. You know it amazes me how much junk we give kids. We can go on teaching the same old stuff over and over and we have the upper hand because we give them the grade and we're the boss. Well, I may not be any brighter than I was before, but at least I think that I'm teaching them more up-to-date material now and at least I feel a little bit better about it. I sometimes think that many kids could do a better job than we do. I don't know. It gets pretty discouraging at times."

That teacher should not be discouraged. Change begins when we face ourselves with the reality that we need to change. The next step is when we accept the reality that we want to do something about it. This teacher faced the need and accepted the responsibility of taking some action.

Shouldn't we all?

WHAT CAN THE TEACHER DO TO CONVERT PRESSURES INTO PROPER MOTIVATION?

As teachers we should all accept the responsibility of taking some action. But how? It is easy to say face pressures, face change, and change. But how? Well, begin with the critics.

The critics of the teacher should inspire him to become more well informed. He should note what the critic is saying, analyze the words in the context of society and then in the context of the School in society and of his role in that society and that School. The teacher should evaluate the critic and extract from his words what appears to be sound and reject what appears to be unsound on the basis of fact not personal emotion, and when that has been done he should forget it. He should use criticism to strengthen his position in implementing many ideas no one would listen to before but now can be documented with the words of an outsider. This can be a powerful tool to help the teacher get across the need for change to a principal, to a superintendent, to curriculum committees, and to other groups looking in on the processes that affect teachers most. He can indicate the social relevancy of change as borne out by the critic, the urgent need to update as brought out by the critic, the awareness that the School is public business, is in the spotlight, and is subjected to the scrutiny of many in all walks of life. He can use the critic as a force to support change, not as an enemy to be shunted aside. The teacher can use the critic as a catalyst for self-directed action not as one who would impose and by so doing threaten. He can use the critic to gain stature, not be forced to withdraw into insecurity.

As for the parent, his pressures can be converted into a challenge to grow, to become more professional. The parent can challenge the teacher to seek greater professional competency, can inspire the teacher to search for more proficiency in his professional abilities and more rational bases for expertise. The parent needs to be viewed as one who can set the sights for change, one who can show how much readiness and acceptance there is for change. How far can the teacher go? What does the parent want? Here, too, the parent can be used as support to achieve ends that might not otherwise be realized. Bring the parent into the process and utilize the energy that is offered as a professional utilizes any resource. Rather than being threatened by it, or overly burdened by it, if the teacher feels secure and feels competent, he can demonstrate these feelings through professional performance. If the teacher is growing in his profession, is searching, is keeping up with the new, is aware of the world, of life, of society, of societal forces, of pressures, of realities; if the teacher is experimenting, is learning new ways, is learning how to use technology, is stretching his mind with new approaches to knowledge; if the teacher is all of this, then no parent can do any more than become one other aspect of professional encounter. Met on a professional level the parent becomes just one more part of a challenge and that challenge can help the teacher. It is all an attitude, a way of thinking about one's position, a way of thinking about one's self, a way of being a teacher, and a way of becoming a teacher in that continual process that is becoming. No finality. Becoming.

Part of such becoming can be a challenge to become better informed. As with the Board of Education, rather than viewing its activities as an external pressure causing painful anxieties over the teacher's performance, he might view the Board as a partner. It is, after all, a partner in the business of operating the schools. If the teacher feels an inward confidence, he should not set the Board up as some fearful sacred cow but should place the Board in its proper perspective of helping in the management of the school system. The teacher would profit from attending the Board meetings that are open to him and, while observing the appropriate professional posture, he would do well to get to know the Board members. I once knew a teacher who invited such individuals into her classroom saying,

> "After all, how are they to help me help the kids if they never get to see any of them in action? Good grief, I don't care if the whole bunch comes into the class. The more the merrier. I want them to know my problems, and they have every right to go where they want, you know. The schools are public property. A lot of teachers forget that, I guess."

And forget it, they do. They forget that the property is an expensive one and that it is one dedicated to excellence on behalf of society. The Board of Education represents that society and it cannot promote excellence unless its interests are being served well with a dollar buying the best that a dollar can. The teacher should become well informed on Board actions, policies, trends, emerging patterns of concern. His professional interests are being determined by that Board and it is a wise teacher who keeps alert. Moreover, more than one teacher has requested permission to speak to the Board, to get his ideas across, to consult with them. It will be a bright day, indeed, when this becomes common practice, when teachers feel comfortable enough to sit with the Board (or have representatives sit in for them), and to consult with the Board on their needs, but more importantly, on the educational needs of children and on the programmatic developments and innovations that could have lasting significance for those children.

As for the pressure to maintain a teacher image, the teacher should not have to turn this on and off. There should be a consistency in his personality, his behavior, and his mentality. What he does and what he represents and what he says and how he presents himself should ring true. This does not refer to those superficials that are part of any person's individuality but refers to the teacher's exemplification externally of his internal being. If the teacher is mentally, physically, morally, and ethically healthy, perhaps the best action for him to take in view of the pressure upon him to maintain some image is for him to reflect the image that is his real self. He can be asked to do no more. He needs to feel that he must express himself and that he is able to do so in reasonably acceptable ways. After all, being committed to the societal need that is teaching, he also needs to be able to compromise some. Should he prefer nudism, for example, he would need to bend to convention and limit his practice of it to his own privacy, for no one could be expected to accept a nude teacher, at least not at this moment. In other words, the teacher has to evaluate the significant issues and distinguish them from those of lesser significance. Not like the teacher who told me,

> "I've resigned. No one is going to push me around like that. When that man [her principal] came in and told me to button my blouse up higher I thought I'd punch him in the gut. That filthy old man. I have a nice body and I'm going to show it. What kid hasn't seen it? They know what the score is. They see their mothers wearing the styles, and I'm not going to look like some weirdo to suit him."

Carrying on and on, she missed the point completely. Her protestations were being spent on issues of lesser priority than she realized. There were no hidden depths to the principal's action. He was not violating her. He was simply asking her to modify for professional discretion the style she had chosen. It was up to her to evaluate whether or not too much of her bosom was showing and to determine whether or not high school boys could learn their American History looking at bare breasts as well as they could looking at covered breasts. If she decided that she could not live with the answer, then perhaps her decision to resign was correct. After all, the teacher is expected to create an image because society wants him to, and when society decides that the teacher can teach naked, then, we are certain, there will be lots of naked teachers. Sometimes, however, to force a trivial point we put ourselves under pressure far more than others put us under it.

As long as there are teachers, as long as there is a school, the students will be a pressure upon the teacher and they should be. Rather than seeing this as a threat or as an annoyance, the teacher should view it as a privilege, hoping to go beyond merely educating to create within the child a respect for teaching itself. The child who respects teaching is linked to one of the most glorious tasks man can know, giving to another through the communication of mind to mind. The teacher must take such pride as well, for he is that link. His mind must be conscious of his student and his consciousness must be attuned to that student's pressures, pressures that become the teacher's challenge to do better, to provide more fully for the needs of another, to give more, to give better. The pressure is the privilege. It is the pressure that comes when one man is close to another, when one man is sensitive to another, when one man knows that another needs him, and needs him at his finest. It is the privilege that few know when they are called upon to serve so completely.

If the privilege is mixed with irritations, it must be expected because the young mind has often not had the experience of educational feedback, has not tasted the rewards of wisdom used. If the privilege is mixed with fatigue, it too must be expected because it is not always easy to give to others. To give is to be drained, but he who has known such giving, such a draining, knows what it means to be alive. If the privilege seems wasted on a stagnant mind or lost in the pressure of the time, it must be remembered that no moment is an entity unto itself but a step toward the hours, the days, the years to come. The song that has been heard is left to be heard again not as a mere echo but as it once was, to be heard again at another time, in another place. The baby's cry is never lost, the deed that was done is never undone. There is no ending, all is a beginning, all is a challenge for that other time of discovery. So it must be with the teacher—never lost, always beginning. Always for another time.

A CASE STUDY

I had withdrawn from the pressures of schedules and scheduling, students and teaching, to the serenity of my own front yard to enjoy the tidying up of late September gardening. The quiet of the afternoon was broken by the urgent tone of my neighbor from down the road, shouting from the street as she came, "Sandy, I've got to talk to you!"

I withstood the impulse to retreat to the house and waited for her to hurry across the lawn to where I stood. A prophet may be without honor in his own land, but not so an educator in his own community.

"I'm sorry," she said. "I know how you guard your time in the yard, but I simply have to talk to you about Ann."

Ann was her youngest daughter, a change-of-life baby, and between being the apple of her daddy's eye and too much to cope with for a no longer young mother, she was spoiled rotten, not so much a "bad" child as an undisciplined, uncontrolled one. Well aware of her failure with Ann, my neighbor had given me all such details more than once. Ann was now in the second grade, in an experimental class with a respected but demanding teacher, Mrs. Thompson—and that was the problem.

"Sandy, as much as I wanted Ann to have Mrs. Thompson, I guess I was wrong. Ann hates her, despises her. She refuses to go to school—says she'll kill herself. She throws up in the morning if I make her go and wets her pants when she does go. I've been at my wits end and———"

"Let her throw up," I interrupted. "She'll get tired of it if you make her clean it up before she goes to school, and let her wet her pants—provided you make her sit there until she's chafed— she'll get tired of that game too." My words poured out unsympathetically, my quick irritation due to Ann's near victory again.

My neighbor's face fell.

"What I mean, Joan," I hurried to inject, already sorry for my impatience, "is that Ann has never met anyone like Mrs. Thompson before. She has never been expected to live up to any standards and no one has ever made her stick to anything."

Joan nodded unhappily as I continued, "What I meant when I told you to let her carry on was that I think you have given in to her too much. If you give in this time you'll just reinforce the old pattern. Mrs. Thompson is the teacher. You should support her and not let Ann get you to take sides against her teacher. That has been the pattern over and over again where authority was concerned. Now that you are aware that something has to be done, do it! I'm just telling you what you already know, Joan."

Tears filled her eyes. "Oh, I know you're right. That's why I came down here as soon as I learned what they had done—to find out what I should do."

"What did *who* do?" I asked.

"The principal moved Ann to another room this morning."

I frowned. "You mean he just up and moved her?"

"As near as I can make out, Sandy, he learned from the school nurse's reports that Ann was throwing up and wetting her pants and missing school, and after talking to some of the other teachers and some of the parents about Mrs. Thompson, he decided to move Ann."

"If he didn't consult you how did you get all this information?"

"From the school nurse. I haven't been able to reach the principal yet. Ann told me when she came home. I wasn't sure what to do, but I did think he should have talked to me first."

"I don't know," I said, not wanting to undermine the principal but still firm in my conviction. "It does seem to me that there should have been a little more investigation that involved you. This is certainly a slap in the face for Ruth Thompson."

"Well, Sandy, if the truth be known, the principal doesn't share your and my regard for Mrs. Thompson anyway, and——"

"Joan," I said, avoiding going into the educational politics of the situation, "take my word for it, Mrs. Thompson is a good teacher, but even if she were just *any* teacher you would be doing Ann a disservice to have her moved."

I spoke as one neighbor to another without considering all the manipulations that might (and did) occur behind what on the surface sounded like such a simple thing—to leave Ann where she was. Later I was to re-evaluate the right of an outsider to meddle, regardless of how right he may be or how much pressure is put on him to do so.

Ann, who started out as the focal point, became only a sidelight to what went on behind the scenes. The real focal point was Ruth Thompson, the teacher. Though I knew her professionally, I did not know that my advice to my neighbor supporting Mrs. Thompson added a final pressure to the many already directed at her—from the superintendent of schools down through resentful teachers to her home itself.

That evening, Tom Hammer, the director of research for our local school system, was at my door. Greetings were brushed over rapidly. "Sandy, what's the lowdown on Ann Lacey being taken out of Ruth Thompson's room?"

"What?"

"Come on, Sandy. I have it from Ruth that you advised Mrs. Lacey to have Ann stay."

Oh God, here we go, I thought.

I gave Tom the story as I knew it. Yes, I had indeed advised that Ann would be better off staying in Mrs. Thompson's room. "But Tom, I didn't intend to get involved in school politics."

"You're not involved. Burns (the principal) should never have moved the child without consulting the parents and investigating further. I'll call the mother now. She and I will meet with Burns and iron this thing out. I can tell you one thing—Ann is going back into Ruth's room. You're right, it's where she belongs."

I didn't feel particularly elated. I had the strong feeling that Ann was being used as a pawn in a power battle between the research director and the principal.

Tom had, before becoming research director, been the principal of Ruth Thompson's school. When he was having a rough time getting started, it being his first administrative job, she had stuck her neck out to help him. Always an aloof type where the staff was concerned, her defense of him made jealous enemies for her when he responded to her as a friend beyond their teacher-principal roles, sharing confidences with her, bragging about her teaching which he thought outstanding, and in general giving her preferred treatment. Things were all right while he was there as principal to protect her from being hurt and to deal with her almost pathological sensitiveness, but when he left the job to become research director, she was left unguarded.

To compound the problem, he had become a member of the Superintendent's Advisory Council of Administrators and in that role vetoed the appointment of his successor as principal, an unfortunate detail that the latter found out. How Hank Burns found out, Tom never learned, but few such secrets are ever kept in education. If Burns held a grudge against Tom and distrusted him, it was equally apparent that Tom considered him an incompetent, unfit to take over what had been *his* school. There was thus no basis for communication between them. Worse yet, there was bad communication between the new principal and Ruth Thompson, who could not disassociate herself from Tom even though he was no longer her immediate superior. She somehow expected him to hold on to the role in absentia, which he was not loath to do, and she gave her loyalty to him rather than to Hank Burns, the man under whom she was supposed to be serving. Some of this Tom reviewed for me before leaving.

Minutes after he left the phone rang. It was Ruth Thompson herself. She told me what was already now obvious: she and Ann's mother had had a long talk on the phone, and she wanted me to know she appreciated the fact that I had gone to bat for her. She had also talked to Tom Hammer, she said, and had tried to work it out for herself, but she was extremely upset and simply had to talk to me. Could she and her husband come over? I said yes and hung up feeling I had unwittingly stepped in quicksand.

Ruth Thompson's husband was still seething when they arrived. He had never wanted her to go on teaching, he told me, but the money factor had overridden his wishes. As the necessity for her to contribute to their budget decreased, his opposition to her teaching increased. She worked too hard at it, he said, and at her age she didn't need all the worry it caused her. She gave more of herself to strangers than to herself or him or their family, and what good did it do? She got the kind of thanks that this present mess illustrated. After all, they had raised three children of their own and the only reason she had gone on to get her teaching certification was because she loved kids. Yet, day after day there was some other irritation. She hadn't even had much time to visit with their son when he came back from overseas duty, but she could give endless time to this Ann's tantrums. Well, he was finished. He'd had it.

Ruth Thompson said her husband did not really know the whole picture because had she told him he would have made her quit long ago. It wasn't just Ann or other children, it was more. With the new principal she couldn't seem to do anything right. He picked on her for the smallest things: not having her class registers in on time, not writing out her reports distinctly enough, not eating lunch with the staff. He made her life miserable. And the other part of it which she never dared tell her husband was that several of her colleagues were bitchy toward her and had been for a long time, in fact ever since her former principal had begun to build her up because of the science fair and the three musical shows she put on. She felt the jealousy of the other teachers and knew their tongues had wagged about her because more than one parent had brought back their stories to her.

Her husband looked at her in disbelief. "That's it, Ruth. Damn it, that's it. I'm the one who has to take care of you when your stomach acts up because you've bolted down your food and then worried for hours afterward about that damn school. I thought it was about the kids and the hard work you do, but it's that bastard in the front office and those bitches you work with. Tell 'em to shove it. You're getting out."

Ruth cried uncontrollably before continuing.

What had happened that morning when the principal had transferred Ann was that she had gone storming down to the principal's office, saying it was the last straw of his many mistreatments of her and demanding to know why she had not been consulted and what he meant by taking a child out of her class. He told her it was not necessary for him to discuss his decisions with her, but that she must be aware that she had a reputation with some of the parents for being too harsh, and that the school nurse's reports of Ann's many absences were evidence that she did not know how to handle the child. He had moved her and she would stay moved, he said.

Ruth was incensed that her reputation as a teacher had been questioned and put on the block. So she did what she had often done before. She went over the principal's head to the research director, Tom Hammer, but not before Ann's mother had called to say that neither she nor I supported Ann's having been moved.

Caught in the middle, all I could do at this point was to sympathize with her, assuring her that her reputation as a teacher was too well established for this to threaten it, advising her to stay calm and allow the administration to handle the situation from here on out. There was no help I could give except to act as a sounding board.

Ann's mother and the research director, Tom Hammer, had their meeting with the principal. My neighbor expressed her wish that Ann be allowed to remain in Mrs. Thompson's room, using the reasons she had discussed with me. Tom backed her up. Burns, caught in a position where his authority was being challenged, refused to reverse his decision. Ann's mother was chagrined and Tom Hammer was furious for now *his* authority was being challenged. Almost simultaneously he and the principal went to the superintendent to register bitter complaints against one another and demand that something be done.

The superintendent called me. He had learned, never mind how, that I knew the facts and he needed an objective point of view. What did I think? After all we were friends and he wanted me to speak freely. It was a tough problem for him that could get out of hand. The truth was, he said, Burns was not doing a good job as principal. Lots of complaints. But then not everybody supported Mrs. Thompson the way Tom had when he was principal, and very frankly, some people did not think so highly of her; she had some very irritating ways.

As for Tom Hammer, said the superintendent, he was having his own problems. He was not only new and uncertain in his role as research director, he was also having trouble letting go of his old school, and informers, if I would forgive the term, like Ruth Thompson, did not help. The school had been Tom's first administrative job and he was like a kid about it, sentimental and all. Also, he did talk too freely at times to old friends and when you're in a job like his you just can't afford to talk to teachers about everything. Keep your ear to the ground but keep your mouth shut was the superintendent's motto.

"Now this is a tough problem," he said. "Here is a parent who was trying to call the shots. She does not want her child moved. She wants her to stay where she was even if she misses half the school year and has to be put back a grade. She feels that her child needs to learn a lesson. She has this under the best professional advice. You can't have the parents running the schools like that. Here's a principal who wants to move that kid out into another classroom where he thinks she would have just as good if not a better experience. Now, the kid's teacher has a tantrum as bad as the kid's. She is being persecuted, she says. She won't stand for it. She goes over the principal's head to the director of research with the advice she's been given that she is good for the child. Now you can't have teachers running the schools either," he said. "They have to take *some* orders. We'd have anarchy if they all went off and did as they wanted. Then you can't have the research director running the principal's school either. He may be caught in the middle of it with the principal bitter against him and the teacher running to him for help all the time, but you can't run a school system like that."

What the superintendent did not say, I felt nonetheless. You can't run a school system with professionals in the community telling parents what to do either. But then, can you expect those same professionals to wear blinders when the administrative personnel and the superintendent himself are caught with their professional pants down? My conscience ached.

The following day the superintendent called a conference with the research director and the principal to give them his decision about the matter. Ann's mother should be granted her request as long as she understood that she had to accept the responsibility if Ann became very ill and/or missed so much school that she would have to be placed back one grade or part of it. That was it. Give it a try. Let the mother try to reinforce in Ann's mind what she, as the mother, felt was needed. Let the mother work it out with the teacher. Perhaps they could accomplish something.

Accomplish they did. Angry, but not wanting to give up until she had won this round, Ruth Thompson put everything she had into making Ann want to come to school and stay in school. Ann's mother supported her and did all that she could to reinforce at home the approaches being used at school. Finally, with time and fortitude, the two women won out over Ann, who came to love school, came to see the teacher as her friend, and made more progress in a few months than most children make in twice that time. On the last day of school before the summer recess Ann cried that she did not want to leave Mrs. Thompson. The mother swore her undying gratitude to the teacher and they promised continued friendship.

Midsummer came and on one of those quiet days of decision, Ruth Thompson wrote out a letter to the superintendent of schools. It was her resignation. She was too tired to go on trying to fight all the battles that have to be fought if one is to teach children. She seemed to have lost her desire to fight.

ANALYSIS

Pressures exist in the ether waiting to be catapulted into a position in which they can exert their power. Such pressures are there for each of us, and for most of us they are the same. They may appear different, but of themselves they are not. Their seeming difference lies in the surrounding circumstances and in our responses as those circumstances stimulate each of us in our individual sensory ways.

As these pressures get into position for catapulting, they drag with them other pressures, for they cannot exist alone. They mingle, they merge into one another, clinging and hovering, surrounding and overtaking. As they are revealed to us, they are revealed to others as well. Even as they are collective themselves, they grab hold of collective victims. They seldom isolate. They give evidence that it is a social world, making us aware that for each pressure we experience someone else is experiencing one also, if not the same pressure, then another because of it.

There is a web woven out of pressures which influence to some degree all they touch until the web becomes thinner and thinner and the impact is finally dissipated. Remaining lie the strangled—those who have not been able to extricate themselves from the web, beyond the catch, and beyond the impact.

4. Teacher Growth through Change

One of the more depressing factors in education is the way administrations often inhibit teacher growth instead of fostering it, often resist change instead of directing it. All too frequently administrators are more concerned with the here-and-now of their tour of duty than with long-range goals or setting the course for future generations. Leadership is often viewed as effective management rather than as educational dynamism, and the teacher becomes just a pawn.

The administration of a school system may merely reflect the needs and readiness of the community it serves instead of reflecting the philosophic commitments of an educational leader and his beliefs about where education is to go and how it is to get there. If significant change is to come, it must often grow out of a painful hassle between the administration and its principles and the Board of Education and its principles. Since administrators often implement decisions made by the Board and execute policies set forth by that Board, they need to exert a forceful voice in the making of those decisions and policies. Unless they do so they become perfunctory servants of the Board rather than educational leaders exercising their abilities as trained professionals. The lay personnel should take their cue from the educator and the educator should act as something more than advisor to lay interests. Ideally, lay and professional should work together to devise the means whereby the world of today is translated into educational language. Too often, much of the relationship between these two groups deals with matters of seemingly more practical and immediate concern. However necessary, this leaves little time for those more profound issues which frequently get lost unless the educational leadership is extremely strong. Whatever the direction, the teacher inherits the pressures that result from the actions of the administration. It is a thoughtless administration that passes along to teachers more pressures than incentives to create. Such incentives when presented must carry with them an environment in which the teacher feels encouraged to experiment, to fail if necessary, with a freedom that reflects his own individuality and with a responsibility for an analysis of his errors. This becomes the major contribution an administration can make. It can help the teacher to become a leader by fostering the commitment to change from within the school enterprise rather than allowing it to become a necessity imposed from without.

If an administration cannot foresee all the implications of change itself, and this perhaps is not its role, it more than ever should sustain an atmosphere in which teachers are given this responsibility. Such change should be outgoing in terms of curriculum revision, instructional revision, administrative provisions for new groupings, staff utilization and the implementation of research findings, and experiments and innovations proposed by the authorities. A school system should remain a laboratory in which new ideas are constantly being tested and, as soon as they show any signs of promise, demonstrated for others, and then disseminated. Every school system should have release time for teachers who are given responsibility for looking into new practices and consulting with teachers, students, and parents about these practices, for drawing up position papers and involving colleagues in dialogues. Teachers should be encouraged to travel to professional meetings and national conventions, encouraged to meet staff from other parts of the country and the world. Teachers should be given the opportunities for becoming leaders, for meeting with professionals in other areas and resource persons of many different types. We cannot expect to get leaders out of organisms who are sequestered within the boundaries of one classroom for an eternity, living off their own energies in parasitic denial. We have to be prepared to allow teachers to become part of a larger world than they customarily experience and we have to give them a stage upon which they may become leaders.

Administration needs to involve teachers in the decision-making process and needs to have their participation in policy level groups. The pattern of open dialogue has to be established so that there is a tone of freedom and a climate of sharing among students, parents, and teachers. Ideally, students and teachers should share, teachers and parents should share, parents and administrators should share and, in turn, each of these should interchange with the others. Such confidence can produce a continuously changing school world wherein new ideas are the expression of people's beliefs and projections of their beings rather than being viewed as fodder for defensive retaliation, manipulations of criticism, and circumstances for hostility. If an educational system expects change as one phase of exemplary performance, then change can become part of the working procedures. If, on the other hand, change is seen as something that simply inconveniences and gets one nowhere, it is denied, apathy takes over, conflicts go underground, and original contribution is inhibited. Too many teachers have gone underground with their courage and their imagination. Too many teachers have suppressed their personalities and their inventiveness. We need to adopt a mentality of orderly revolution in education and not make a sacred cow of our past successes or create a defense of our numerous past failures.

At no other time has the raw material for excitement in education been so available. We need to make of technological advances, curricular experiments, public interest, and other such components a way of life and not continue to evoke innovation as a condemnation of institutionalized education. Administrations must establish the standard that change is honorable and must not make iconoclastic views appear disloyal. There must be an atmosphere of divergence, and from among the numerous variables we must choose the most promising denominators. If this is not done willingly then other factors will tend to take the privilege away from administrations. These are the factors of new power coalitions.

THE POWER GROUPS

One of the more flamboyant aspects of change in the teacher's world is the emergent uses of collective power. Three separate power groups threaten to change the very foundations of education and should be dealt with while they can still be utilized as positive energy. They will not be stopped. The choice appears to be whether they will be used cooperatively or become independent forces. They are teacher power groups, parent power groups, and student power groups.

During recent months we have been witness to many events which herald the dawn of a new day when people will not stand still waiting for others to direct the course of their lives. Teachers have been ready to jeopardize their professional standing, to pick up the picket-line placard and protest everything from working conditions to the very children they teach, from salary levels to the hours they work, from the paper work they must do to the parents with whom they must deal. They have formed a large labor force that wants an equal share of the taxpayers' loot. They strike, they advertise, they bargain, they vote on their causes, they withstand public abuse. They scream out their new found power and say that if the observer sees it as it is, he will realize the teachers have now forced administration to deal with them as a force powerful enough to take control of their conditions if some part of that control is not given to them. For the first time in the history of education, the teacher is assuming a different relationship to the power lines established by tradition.

But teachers are not alone. The parents are moving into their own new power position. They will not stand by and wait for the voice of the school people. They want a voice of their own and this is a voice that could shatter many of our preconceived notions about what the parent is to do. For decades that notion has not included the possibility that parents would want a voice in curriculum decisions, in instructional decisions, in hiring practices and the selection of teachers, in the management of the schools, and in general policy-making. But they want these things now. The parental power movement is with us and it will snowball as America realizes that social change cannot come about without educational change, and that as the schools have failed in a leadership role regarding much social change, they cannot be allowed to fail again. Hence, the patrons of the schools must assume greater power.

The students, too, are moving into educational power relationships. They are coming more and more to demand a partnership with the professionals over those matters that concern them the most, and they are capable of exercising their power with violence. As parents picket and protest in ways not dissimilar from teachers, students are apt to stage sit-in demonstrations, close down school operations, and prevent personnel from entering or leaving jobs. Student power is becoming a force that could be disruptive beyond all precedent unless ways are devised to bring it into constructive focus.

The School establishment appears destined not to be able to go its own way without involving those most concerned with the results of its activities: teachers, parents, and students. Unless brought into proper perspective, the situation tends to suggest that the present state of education is due to undergo so drastic an alteration as to be shattered from without before it has time to accommodate itself from within.

The tragedy of all this is that too few are aware of what is happening and too few seem to care. The many stand to lose for want of a leadership that can interpret the events of change. Could not and should not that leadership in change begin with the teacher himself and the understanding of what being a teacher can mean?

WHAT IT CAN MEAN TO BE A TEACHER

To be a teacher can mean to help bring to life the sleeping potential within another human being. It can mean to have faith in a universal plan, in ideals that contribute to it, and in the boys and girls who are a part of it. It can mean to give of oneself and to love the giving and love the one who receives. It can mean to cast light upon this life that is a journey and not a destination.

To be a teacher can mean to beckon to each child to reach his thoughts toward unknown horizons and to guide him in finding peace within himself this day and always. To be a teacher can mean fulfilling self by helping others fulfill themselves.

To do this, to reach his greatest potential, the teacher needs to become well aware of the numerous crises facing the human race: overpopulation, food shortages, depletion of natural resources, conquest of disease, radiation dangers, nuclear stockpiles, competition in space, survival itself. We tend to read about the threats, talk about them, even worry over them, but in our own way we all too often dismiss any further obligations with such conscience-salving devices as optimism, defeatism, or the feeling that as individuals we are too small to cope with the problems anyway. What is needed now more than at any other time in our history, even as much as at the very inception of our nation, is a renaissance of individual initiative. We await, and the veritable continuation of our way of life awaits, the re-emergence of individual responsibility.

With dramatic certainty we who are teachers touch the future with our very presence. It is our individual initiative that can lead the way. And is our touch marked with conviction? Is it punctuated with principles, standards, values that reflect the best in living? Do we know where we are going and does the path we take exemplify character? Are we aware of the fact that what we teach today must mature and develop in order to flourish as tomorrow's thought? To present today for itself alone is not enough.

And while facing today with a positive outlook on life can be healthy, optimism as an end within itself can prove to be a dangerous blindfold over reality and truth. Optimism needs to be founded upon facts, and the facts are not always comfortable. As teachers aware of the facts, we must gain a point of view that broadens our perspective beyond the limitations of our immediate environment and service. We need to expand our vision to the dimensions that are far out and away. This means that we must see ourselves as a part of the world and the world as being constructed of just such individuals as ourselves. We need to see ourselves as contributing in mind and deed to a world arena, as inspiring and challenging the future. In many instances this means we have to overcome our own mental state of inertia. We have to awaken from a tragically national lethargy. As teachers, we can begin to do this for ourselves through a concerted program of reading, studying, and exploring the most effective use of consultants and research findings, and by soul-searching.

The role of the teacher is a changing one. It changes as the world about us changes. Day by day our responsibility to accept the challenges of the world of which we are a part intensifies. We cannot wait. We cannot justify what we are not doing from the standpoint of what once was done. We cannot justify from the standpoint of what we have not learned, do not know. We have to do, we have to learn, we have to know: we have to change with change. What our American way of life is to become and what the world is to become are issues for us to act upon. We cannot close our consciences and delegate our obligations to the politician, the scientist, the businessman—to anyone. Life requires a working team and we are an integral part of that team. There is no time for complacency. Our voice must be heard, not in the role of a small frightened servant but in an historic role of dignity and honor. The teacher is an educator, the practitioner of the most glorious of all professions. We must not let our great era of service, our call to act upon the forces of society go down to defeat. We must not fail. We cannot fail. As the need intensifies, so we must intensify our efforts. The challenge is all around us, and as teachers we must act. We must act upon traditional attitudes and establish within the core of our beings the awareness that we have a responsibility to move toward the enlightenment that must come if the world of democratic principles is to survive. We must provide the sort of quality education that is real for today, that will be functional for tomorrow. It must be provided in view of what we now know about the mind, what we now know about human growth, and what we hold to be the cardinal educational goal, developing and training the whole individual for a contributing role as a moral citizen in society.

It is not enough to keep order in our own particular classroom, to teach the prescribed pattern to our own particular students experimenting only here and there where the course of study is either inadequate or has been exhausted. We cannot mirror the image of a working group who only punch in and punch out, begrudging the necessity for additional expenditures of time and energy. We cannot content ourselves with being the dispensers of a duplicative machinery of methods devised for the needs of other times, any more than we can content ourselves to dispense a curriculum designed around yesterday's beliefs, facts, and achievements. In fulfilling our obligation to teach the history and development of those elements that make up the present, we must establish for ourselves a value structure which includes a positive commitment to the best possible use of our time and the time of our students. We must see ourselves from the standpoint of our worth to the desperate need we fill.

Is all this idealistic? Yes, admittedly so. But must we continue to look upon ideals as being unattainable? Must the status quo so overwhelm us that we feel there is no hope for positive change? Must we become submerged under the weight of the moral dilemma so apparent in today's youth? Must we settle for a generation who cannot think critically, who cannot deal with basic human actions with the dignity and pride of spiritual beings rather than as animals who weaken the core of existence with a lack of intrinsic ethics and morality?

What does this idealism have to do with what it can mean to be a teacher? Everything. At the foundation of all the teacher does should be the understanding that he is doing this for life, for horizons beyond his own. Before he can teach with the power to lead forth he must know more than his own specific goals. He needs to project beyond himself, beyond the particular age group with which he works. He needs to see the ultimate, eventual needs, and he needs to direct his own energies to moving toward what must lie ahead. He must be vital beyond individual personality, individual methods. He must be vital because he must impart knowledge, must train minds, must open up the ongoing experiences of a lifetime to the boys and girls who will become the men and women of tomorrow. They will inherit the problems, fears, failures, as well as the challenges and successes he has helped to create. How they will contribute, grope, search; how they will live, think, and succeed begins now, with him. They are never too young. The present will become the future with frightening rapidity. What they are to become begins now. It begins with definite measures to insure the best possible mental, emotional, physical, moral, and spiritual development. That growth is assured is a known fact; the type of growth and the results are not assured. This is the challenge inherent in the teacher's role.

Although that role in society is a changing one, it has a base of operations that begins with the teacher's own attitude. He must see himself and know himself so that he may discover where his responsibility to society lies and how he can pay his obligations. As every world citizen should, he must search deep and long within himself and know his weaknesses and strengths. To do this he might look at the teacher who epitomizes the full meaning of the title "teacher" and ask himself, "How do I measure up?"

THE CONSUMMATE TEACHER

What then is the consummate teacher? He is a commentator on the events of life as illuminated by his discipline. He is one who deploys the skills of his discipline as a collaborator playing with ideas. He is both director of and participant in the experiences he shares with his students, moving skillfully, even rhythmically, from the role of choreographer to that of performer among his learners.

Peter Abelard in the twelfth century proclaimed the power of human reason to achieve through knowledge. In his *Ethica* he wrote:

> Knowledge is the conquering of our resistant powers so that we might show responsiveness to ideas and the expression of them.

This is what makes a teacher a teacher. He learns to overcome his own resistant powers and how to respond to knowledge in such a way as to be capable of challenging the resistant powers in others.

This teacher is wise. Pico della Mirandola said in the fifteenth century, "we shall live forever, not in the schools of wordcatchers, but in the circle of the wise." So then this teacher becomes one of that circle in which, by his actions, he may offer to others their own dignity. As Mirandola said in his *Dignity of Man:*

> Whatever seed each man cultivates will grow and bear fruit in him. If these seeds are vegetative, he will become like a plant; if they are sensitive, he will become like the beasts; if they are rational, he will become like a heavenly creature; if intellectual, he will be an angel and a son of God.

This consummate teacher is a synthesizer. He goes to the sources of knowledge and makes use of them. He interprets knowledge in terms of the needs of his own age and is a potential creator of new wonders out of the old. This has been a process in all the great advances of civilization. During the Renaissance the early leaders of the humanist movement went to the Greek and Roman classics for stimulation. Others like Mirandola went to the Oriental, the Hebrew, the Arabic.

This teacher is one who contributes to the progress of civilization. He awakens and brings to a conscious level ideas which had been dormant. He provides a bridge between the present and the coming ages. He sees life as an art and is capable of expressing its forms through various rhythms. He helps developing minds become aware of Descartes' theory, "I am a thing which thinks." He also helps those same minds to become aware of Bergson's, "I am a thing which continues."

This teacher involves himself with the process of the making of the man. He accepts the challenge of helping learners develop those qualities of thinking and of continuing that are a part of all men. This teacher assimilates the challenges, the ideas, the events, the changes in life, and evaluates these according to his own ethics, his own values, his own commitments, his own knowledge. Then he disseminates. He uses his professional training to disseminate to others those experiences he deems necessary and worthy of being passed on—for his own fulfillment and for the fulfillment of his students.

Where does this teacher begin? Accepting the challenge that what he does is for tomorrow as well as for today, he analyzes what he ought to be doing today. Accepting the challenge that he must see himself as part of the world, he analyzes what he can do to strengthen this position.

The consummate teacher uses outstanding education as his basic ingredient—outstanding education, which means the creating of a climate, the establishing of an environment wherein opportunities are made available for the development of personality and character. This, rather than the environment of a workroom, is where this teacher molds raw material. This molding takes place within the individual students and it increases as their readiness and motivation are established. As a teacher then, he inspires the student to move toward the expression of his own uniqueness, his own thinking and doing. As a teacher he releases potential that makes possible a gradual fulfillment of the student's inner being. He lights fires from which the student's true self emerges aflame.

This teacher provides experiences that offer breadth and depth of personal thought and deed to the student. He allows each child the opportunity to expand in the way that is natural to him, and he teaches the child to evolve his own methods of dealing with facts, problems, and skills. This forms the basis upon which all the child's future independent action will be built. He is careful not to so structure and control the child's every action that he inhibits true expression of self. Nor does he allow the child's self-expression to be limited to art, music, and the crafts, for self-expression is vital to all thought. This teacher pursues outstanding education and outstanding education accents independent action. It also presents the young person with a reason for attaining skills. Outstanding education offers an inside look at the very nature of learning, and attempts to train the mind to deal with the structure of the disciplines of knowledge, its logic, skills, and functions. Outstanding education inspires an appreciation of the history of human achievement, offers opportunities for the grasp of ethical, spiritual, aesthetic, and moral values. It sets the stage upon which critical thought may be voiced, and extends the awareness of the social and personal responsibility of each individual, leading the child toward the ability to handle knowledge in a way that provides him with a key to a continuing experience of learning and growing. Outstanding education supports its claims of being outstanding by giving substance to every experience, and by making each experience meaningful, practical, and developmental. What is taught in the third grade ought to be meaningful when the pupil reaches the thirteenth grade.

The success of outstanding education will be measured by the continuity and sequence of skills and experiences it has provided. The education of each young person ought to appear to him to have a feeling of totality. There should be security in the knowledge that all the many threads weave together, that though the cloth will never be finished, there is an order, a pattern, a plan.

The consummate teacher is the catalyst for such an education. He inspires it, he exemplifies it, he moderates it, he accepts its objectives as his major responsibility. Committed to quality, this teacher becomes the key that unlocks doors for each child. In a sense, this teacher brings the world to the child and gives it to him as a creation in such a way that the child feels stimulated to think for it and to create for it. This teacher takes the qualities which exist within each learner and nourishes them. To do this he has to realize that thought itself is like a passage leading toward light. He has to analyze what the appropriate means are by which he can emphasize conscious thinking on the part of the child in all that child does.

In 342 B.C. Philip of Macedon appointed Aristotle the tutor of his young son, Alexander. In *Metaphysics,* Aristotle says to young Alexander:

> Education must be the arrangement of thought, the triumph of logic which produces clarity and orderliness. Education makes possible the power to create, to systematize, to arrive at greater knowledge by reasoning from what is known.

This consummate teacher heeds the words of Aristotle, then, as John Milton prescribed, "takes his exceptional gifts and puts them to uses of service for others."

WHAT CAN THE TEACHER DO ABOUT CHANGE?

In "On Education," written in 1644, Milton wrote that one should not be imprisoned within himself. This must apply to teacher and student alike. And the teacher who is not aware of change and how to use it does become imprisoned within himself and threatens to imprison his students.

In 1894, after realizing that his publishing company had failed and that he was bankrupt, Mark Twain said to his friend William Dean Howells, editor of the *Atlantic Monthly,*

> I failed but I keep right on learning. Growing old is growing wiser and if there is one thing I know it is this. What's the use of growing if you can't sit down and rebuild the world in your thoughts? It might be no better than the one you're living in now, but it's yours. You build it. What's the mind for if you can't dream a little?

Unlike Mark Twain, many a teacher has not gone right on learning. Faced with change, he has not tried to rebuild the world in his own thoughts or as a result of his own actions. He has not dreamed enough. Rather, he has been the receiver, the follower, the one everything happens to. What can he do about change? How can he be the doer and not the done to? Having evaluated his potential against a consummate teacher, he can unify his energies toward the activation of his own personal resources: he can look toward the training or retraining of his mind. With a mind competently trained, the teacher will face himself with greater security as he faces change with less insecurity. Such training will reduce his fear of change by placing him in contact with the learning recorded in the annals of the history of education. Here is a magnificent storehouse of knowledge upon which the teacher can base his reactions, methods, experimentation, and rejections. He should see in it the whole panorama of human experience and profit from the great legacy left him by time and the men who lived it. The teacher must build upon history while he makes history himself.

Although change has gained new impact in our time because of its rapidity, its variety, and its possibilities for global communication, change has been a constant throughout all ages. And teachers studying the past in order to understand the present should relate both the past and the present to the future. Then perhaps they can see the enormous opportunities in change. Perhaps then they can view change as an arrow-like vehicle to speed the mind on exhilarating journeys that can be related to all other mental journeys traveled. Perhaps then they can have a vision of ways in which they can rise above the limitations of immediacy, escape the bonds of time and superficial dimensions, and fashion for themselves their own world of reality. Only such a course can set the direction that inspires teachers to train youth to produce for a changing society. Such a direction must be set for the world we all would like to help construct through the positive uses of change.

TRAINING THE MIND THROUGH HISTORY

The history of education itself is a history of how various ages pursued the training of the mind in ways deemed valuable by the existing standards. Society prescribed areas of training in a hierarchical order to produce the results that were deemed of greatest value. Hence, in ancient Greece the ideal of education was to train the good man to become the good citizen. Knowledge was pursued for its own sake, its ultimate good directed toward its use for the state.

In Quintilian's *Institutio Oratoria,* we are able to read about the development of Roman education and its genesis from emphasis upon *grammatici,* the teaching of grammar and literature, to formalization of rhetoric and philosophy. Quintilian saw the decline in Roman education as paralleling the weakening of morals and the loss of the family as an educational example. There is much here that is provocative to us today as we analyze the moral tone of the home as well as the school.

Christianity saw its first educational responsibility as a training in the faith, but gradually it came to be felt that the best direction to its philosophy could be found in liberal culture. In this way faith could be attained intellectually. Clement of Alexandria was the leader of this movement and though it came under attack, it still continues as an influence upon the progress of education. Again and again, leaders have returned to the idea that the supremacy of man's nature and the fulfillment of his destiny can be expressed best through intellectual achievement. Through the centuries there have been many variations upon this essential theme. The theme was there in the medieval curriculum of the trivium and the quadrivium with their elaborate emphasis upon the content and form of literature and the formal logic of dialectics. Another time the theme came forth in the syllogistic logic of the thirteenth century Scholastics, a movement that led to the foundation of the universities of Western Europe.

With the Italian Renaissance came the rise of the spirit of education that so permeates our thinking today, the assertion of the individual. The Italian Humanists glorified the heritage of knowledge and combined this with an inspiration to create thought in an atmosphere of intellectual freedom, personal integrity, and individual conviction. We see the restatement of the worth and self-reliance of the individual, the pleasures of existence, the supremacy of human intellect and realities to be found in classical studies.

The story of education is the story of man's progress, his recognition of his spirituality, his groping for the meaning in and the purpose of life, his reaching toward the better life, realizing a fulfillment of his own dreams. It is a long story and, while not always a pleasant one, it chronicles man's moving toward action based upon refinement of mental processes over and above the responses of other mammals.

Some believe that as we set our goals toward physical comfort and find the purpose of productivity to be an easier way of life, we lose the base fiber of man's initiative which, it is argued, grows out of needs and conflicts. We cannot turn back the clock of progress and convenience, nor would we want to, but we cannot allow materialistic comfort to cause an atrophy of man's most powerful tool, his mind. The great teachers of the world, Moses, Socrates, Jesus, Buddha, were able to lead men to a greater use of mind in order to bring about change at moments in history when the future of civilization was to be determined.

To define education is to deal in the intangibles of what happens to man, what springs from within him, what he does. All this is visible in the great interaction with life forces and other people. Moreover it involves dealing in the intangibilities of a potent essence that can transform men and their habits, alter customs, and create traditions.

The teacher must become a pioneer in change, one who understands it and works with it and for it, comprehending while shaping it. The teacher cannot become apathetic in the sanctity of tenure or negligent in the power-engendering atmosphere of a picket line. The teacher cannot look backward but must go forward facing the inevitabilities of change and the awesome needs for change if civilization is to flourish.

PREPARING FOR CHANGE

But again what can one teacher do about change? Again, he can prepare. He can prepare himself to view change with a mentally healthy approach. Instead of acquiring the posture of one who is uninformed and threatened, he can map out a course for himself which can head him in positive directions. There are numerous possibilities in pursuing specialized and quality college offerings in such areas as computer technology, programming, audio-visual instruction, group dynamics, individualized instruction, learning theories, communications media, race and minority relations, Soviet-American relations, non-Western studies, learning through inquiry, and many others. Some courses of this type provide insights into methodology and most especially into techniques for manipulating content, while other courses provide challenges in fields which the average teacher either has not explored or has explored without sufficient depth. The teacher's mind cannot change unless it has a cultivated awareness of various dimensions of learning. All too many teachers come to be limited as much by the restrictive uses they assign to what they do know as by what they do not know.

Another direction might be that of in-service training. Unfortunately, most in-service training appears to be introduced by the administration rather than by teachers requesting it. And when introduced, much of it becomes caught up in the dilemma of when it will be offered, will there be salary increments for it, and will it carry career credits along with it? Regrettably we seem headed toward a position where the materialistic concerns of teachers threaten to push aside those intrinsic values so necessary for professional growth. Perhaps it is naive to believe that whether or not certain other factors such as salary and the like were included, the teacher should ask for the kinds of in-service training that would make him better prepared to deal with the issues of change. But, provided there is release time for the teacher, there should be so great a motivation to learn and to grow on his part that the values of the intellectual involvement should outweigh all other elements.

Change for the teacher begins right in his classroom. Here is where the teacher has his power. Whatever the decision-making process in any school system, the final decision is made by the teacher in his classroom. He selects, he interprets, he modifies, he changes. Unfortunately, too many teachers are unaware of this power and too many of those who are aware of it do not use it at all. Yet the power is there and it is a reality to be reckoned with. Whatever the decision at the Board of Education offices, the teacher has the last word. Hence, that word can subtly and with responsibility bring about desirable change. The teacher can make this change take place through the individual changes he makes in his instruction, his curriculum, through the ways in which he uses curriculum as an instrument. For the teacher, his instruction becomes his ministry. It can be overt and powerful. It can present alternatives without editorialization. The teacher must be unafraid of controversy or of becoming liable to criticism. Provided he dispatches himself and his ideas with integrity, honesty, and morality, he must stand up for his convictions based upon the knowledge he has acquired, the skills he has developed, and the results he has achieved.

For the teacher who is aware of the urgencies of the world, aware of the changes that have evolved, of those areas of life which are changing, aware of change itself, there is no one who can stop him from adjusting his classroom activity to reflect all this awareness. He will respond and will demonstrate this response in his own attitudes, actions, and expectations.

When something more than classroom modification of the curriculum and adjustment of teaching styles is warranted, then the teacher must investigate drawing up a proposal for actual curricula revision. Such a proposal should be based upon research evidence and should be developed with precision and documentation of sources of reference. Substantiated by such authority and demonstrating commitment, this proposal can then be presented to principal and supervisor for discussion and eventual approval.

Such a written proposal for change can avoid the circumstance of a teacher being placed in a posture of challenging the administration. And if the teacher bases his beliefs upon his consistent classroom behavior he will get support for his style from the enthusiasm of his students and from the success he has with them. Such results will also win parental support. After all, parents soon become aware of the good things as well as the bad, and they can be powerful allies. Any school system that does not honor such a proposal for change is not one wherein individual initiative is respected. With such handwriting on the wall the teacher has the issues clearly stated: *Status quo or Go.* There is no question about it, many teachers put to the test choose the status quo path. Fortunately many others choose the pathway of dedication to principles and although it may mean Go or in any case is rarely a path strewn with roses, it is in the long run the way to greater honor and greater satisfaction.

In my own experience I pursued such a course. When I taught public school not too many years ago, I came to believe after much painful deliberation that the gifted students were not getting the best education possible. Much study and research led to the presentation of evidence to the superintendent of schools. He allowed his assistant to take over the matter and I, in turn, was allowed to travel to various school systems to investigate programs and to interview authorities in the field of the gifted. It was this trip, in fact, that led to my first meeting with three of America's leading specialists on the gifted. As a result of this meeting I was invited to share the teaching of a practicum on the education of the gifted at a New York college, a big challenge for a classroom teacher. The results of this trip led to a report on practices for the gifted and to recommendations for the implementation of its provisions. These latter resulted in my being released from classroom duties and moving into central Board of Education offices to prepare a guide for the education of the gifted for the school system. As this work progressed, I was appointed to a new position as consultant to the school system on programs for the gifted. This entailed establishing a committee whose task was to study the system-wide implications on various grade levels of my recommendations, the strategy of a teacher and administrator training program, the grouping of students according to criteria of selection that had been assigned, and consultative contacts with those classes, the staffs of the buildings, students, and parents. In other words, because I as a classroom teacher sought change, the school system moved into a program and I moved into a different role. This was made possible by the confidence and imagination of the assistant superintendent who had been recently promoted to superintendent of schools.

A footnote must include the sad fact that the effort had its demise when the superintendent of schools failed to get support for the program as a change concept. He failed to get support for it and other programs he had developed because the Board of Education, in an austerity campaign to save dollars by running the school system like a supermarket business, assigned a price tag to all school programs and delegated priorities of expenditure. Yet, although the approach failed for want of money, the experience proves that just one teacher can do something and can have an impact. If other factors move in to disrupt the dream, nonetheless we can live with our own conscience as we formulate our convictions, uphold these, and make ourselves vulnerable because we care.

Schoolteachers are not exempt from the human frailty of suffering when life and death judgment is passed on their dreams. Sometimes the thumbs down on a dream is the result of small minds passing superficial judgment, and sometimes it is the result of inquiring minds seeking more universal or more immediate goals. And sometimes even established changes are thrown out the window when the man in the driver's seat leaves and a new boss moves in. As stated at the beginning of this chapter, not all administrators know how to give their teachers the opportunity to grow. Too many such administrators have held teachers back because anything new threatened their equilibrium and kept them from pushing around their schedules and paper clips without interruption. If the going gets too rough with such a mentality at the helm, move on. There are too many spots for energetic teachers today, and no one with spirit should allow that spirit to get broken at the feet of one less interested in dynamics than in being loved by his Board of Education in order to protect his own paycheck. Move on. That may be the first big step in change that the teacher needs to take and all others may unfold as a result.

But whatever the outcome, as teachers we cannot stop our energies because we may meet with rebuff or may get our feelings hurt or may have to move on. We have to live with the hope that as we act to change, we will be allowed the opportunity to influence others through our efforts. Whatever direction his path leads, the alert, professional teacher has to decide that he will become a catalyst for change, that he will embrace the challenges that confront him. He has to present himself as a spokesman for the contemporary arena of activity, has to manifest the qualities of personality and professionalism that indicate his readiness to become part of the vanguard leading change. The teacher cannot remain the constant recipient of other people's mandates. He has to mandate for himself. He cannot remain the recipient of other people's commitments. He has to be committed himself. The teacher has to express himself as a person and cannot remain a name on a schedule. He has to be someone to reckon with. He cannot become depersonalized. He must stand up for his humanity—now. Tomorrow may be too late. He has to become a part of change and as he changes he will continue to be changing and in the process he will continue to be a person moving toward fulfillment and will continue to grow in that state of becoming.

It is a strange thing that teachers have to be encouraged to face change with courage because they live with it daily. The child they teach is not static and yet many teachers become static while working with him. The baby flesh covered by baggy trousers and woolen sweaters hardens into muscle by the time the playground has been washed clean by April rains. The wobbly curves of the pubescent girl, uncertain of line and less sure of intention, melt into soft contours of awakened woman. The days pass from Halloween into Christmas, from Valentine's Day on to Easter, while the lessons go on and the changing child goes on changing. And before too long the child of yesterday is the adolescent sitting there giggling at the mention of a girl or blushing at the word "love." And the teacher has lived with it, seen it, found its challenges, and accepted its inspiration.

The world of change as a revolution of body growth and mental expansion is an accepted process. Can it be that teachers grow so accustomed to heaven's first law of order they fail to see that change erupts out of order only to put things back into changed order again? Can it be that teachers who deal with change every day find it too uncomfortable in others to want to experience it for themselves? Or do they see it no further than activity for the glands and the days of youth? Do they·come not only to accept but to strive for the status quo that brings with it the known, the less volatile, and the more comfortable?

What a pity that at the very place where students' bodies and minds are experiencing the force of change most dramatically so many teachers' minds and spirits are congealing with the inertia of bland acceptance. What a misfortune that when students are preparing to scale the heights of ambition, too many teachers who might inspire and lead them allow themselves to settle on a plateau of ennui. What a tragedy these teachers do not free the laboratories of their minds by facing the daily facts of outward change with the equally exciting and more fascinating pursuit of inward change. What a pointless waste that such a provocative invitation to live should be refused by so many.

5. Design for Change

Design. Reason. Plan. Purpose. Design.

Why should change be different? Why should we not design it with reason? Why should we not plan for it with purpose? Why not a design for change?

What alternative is there? A lack of design. The danger of destructive action as opposed to constructive action is ever present. The danger of apathy overcoming energy is ever present as well. The possibility of misplaced efforts, duplicated efforts, unrelated efforts is ever present. The possibility of poor communication, poor leadership, poor guidance is ever present. The problems of no impact and of no continuity are ever present as well. Design is needed.

A design gives momentum to the need for change. A design places change on a plane with any other area in which a blueprint is prepared with comprehensive concern for all those separate elements that must of necessity be a part of a larger construct. Design gives guidelines for the dimensions of the final composite. It calls attention to all details because one is dependent upon another and because each is necessary for the support of the total. It provides for the foundation, for the internal make-up, for the operativeness. It is a commitment, a creative direction. It is a goal. It is a way of reaching that goal. It is fluid. Its opposite, a lack of design, leaves no way except the way that is without plan, without overall purpose, without control, without faith that change can be managed by man, can be utilized as an attribute, as a force through which man can express his beliefs, his personality, and, above all, can give testimony to his basic character and principles. A design is an act of humanity. A lack of design is a lack of regard for progress. A plan is courageous. The absence of one is weakness.

Change will take place anyway. What choice is there? Design for change or be overpowered by it and too weakened to contend with it as the demands of tradition, comfort, leisure, and lethargy sap the potential for greatness within each of us.

This is a time marked by dramatic societal changes on all sides. Technology is transforming the fabric of our lives as we find science reducing infant mortality and increasing the life expectancy of adults, providing us with more leisure time and shooting us toward space. This is the age of accelerated capital accumulation with resultant increases in industrialization, urbanization, and rapid mobility. It is an age of expanding uses of communication, the sharing of cultures, and the potential for understanding world events. At no other time in history has man been more challenged in his responses to change. He has come to see a discord within the structure of the family, a discord in the dialogue between the generations, a discord in the emergent alterations in relationships between the sexes. Man has come to see the tensions in racial injustice, in national disunity, in national and international conflicts, in wars. This is an age in which man is constantly being subjected to an assault upon his senses through the provocations of advertising, commercialism, and communications. He is being challenged to look beyond himself into a world beyond his own needs, a world where there is prejudice, where there is poverty, where there is horror, and where there is terror. Man is becoming more and more aware that all do not share the economic strength of middle-class white Americans. All men do not enjoy psychological peace. All do not enjoy social peace. For too many in this age life is filled with uncertainties. This is an age of pressure, an age of anxiety.

TASKS FOR THE SCHOOL

The School as an institution is affected by each of these societal changes and by the tone of all social change, whether it be actual or attitudinal. As a result of such changes, there are certain tasks the School must perform if it recognizes its role in society and if it does not want to forestall the inevitable.

The School must move toward a position where the effects it has experienced as a result of societal changes become a part of consciousness. Only where such effects are a conscious part of the School's mentality in terms of where it stands in relationship to the world and to society can it begin to face clearly the prospects of designing programs and administrative provisions to incorporate change. The School cannot go on pretending that change does not affect it nor that change will not change it nor that change can somehow or other remain subliminal. Change has to become a part of the conscious modus operandi of the School; then and only then will it become a healthy element to be used constructively.

The School must move toward an ability to assess the significance of the effects change has upon it. As with any organism, and the School is in so many ways a living matter, that which has effect upon it must be assessed in terms of its significance relative to the School's present course, the School's response to the effect, and the School's future strategies. Since these strategies might well be developed out of such assessment, it is appropriate that the School give top priority to the more immediate and necessary change elements and lower priority to less significant change elements. Such a procedure for assessment of significance and the assignment of priorities of concern is necessary for avoiding confusion or the helter-skelter weakening of efforts and is a prerequisite to the rudiments of design. Such an approach testifies to the School's conscious awareness of the effects of social change upon it and shows it to be in control of assessing the significance of such change. This is a leadership response.

The School must move toward a position where it can study the ways in which it can respond to societal changes. As a result of its conscious awareness of such change and as a result of its assessment of the significance of these changes upon it, the School now needs to move into an active study of the ways in which it can respond to the effects of change philosophically, administratively, attitudinally, programmatically, developmentally. Viewing the priorities of significance and involving itself in a specific program of research and analysis relative to the effects of change, the School can determine methods and strategies for response. Thus, it will control response and make it a part of the School's commitments. By doing this, it can also reject response, but only after moral deliberation and not because of negligence. The School can then be respected for decisions based upon its research and guided by intellectual considerations as opposed to emotional ones.

The School must move toward a position where it can propose direct recommendations for action on the basis of study and can proceed to evaluate those recommendations in terms of their merit, their urgency, their moral intentions, and their contribution to the greater society. Such evaluation can involve consultants of many sorts and should involve parents and interested citizens. It should be pointed out to all citizens that they stand to benefit each time the School, through such careful probing, moves to incorporate that which it feels it must and it can of change. Such action will place the School in a dynamic relationship to change. And although it cannot stop societal changes, it will be acting to control some of its own responses to such changes through consciousness, assessment of significance, study, and evaluation.

CHOICES THAT CONFRONT THE SCHOOL

Such tasks are an exciting aspect of design for change and as a result of them the following choices will confront the School.

The School can decide to reject a change factor outright. Based upon careful consideration the School can determine through its study and evaluation that it will reject some aspect or other of change or even some whole segment of it or some entire impact of it. For example, although communications media are causing a widely changing concept of instruction through the uses of much multi-media equipment and approaches, the School can decide to reject this. Although conscious of it and although having assessed its significance, it might have studied the implications of the vast expenditures required to respond to such a practice and may have reached the opinion that the money might more profitably be spent in the hiring of some additional professional staff to relieve the teachers who are ready to move into a team teaching situation. Such rejection, then, is conscious and determined on the basis of having assigned priorities to strategies, and it is done after honest and moral judgment. Such a position can be respected if not necessarily agreed with, and perhaps all that anyone can expect to garner during such frenetic times is the respect of their colleagues. All schools will not take the same course but all should be respected for judgments that have come of introspection and self-searching.

The School can decide to adjust to change as something that is occurring outside its physical plant but can agree to do nothing about it educationally. For example, aware of the pressures of civil rights groups for integration, it may adjust to the conscious awareness that it will be affected by concerns for interracial justice; but it may decide to adjust to these through an acceptance of their importance. Then, based upon study and evaluation, it may decide that there is no educational direction warranted in response to those concerns for interracial justice. Here is an example where change can vary in its significance and its level of priority from location to location. Although all schools should study the events around the civil rights revolution—and it would be inconceivable to imagine any school in America not immediately placing the life and death of Dr. Martin Luther King in its curriculum—not all schools would have the same needs regarding integration. Some schools would determine that quality education where the student is would be the best approach. Some schools would be distant from various racial groups because of geographical location. Some schools would be crossed off the list by the racial groups themselves as places to integrate. There are many variables and the point is that any school can adjust to change but can determine through intellectual processes not to incorporate a change educationally. In this regard, it is important to note that this process is a continual one: decisions made today must be evaluated again tomorrow so that contemporary thinking is apparent in school policy at all times. The day when decisions made at a Board meeting in August of one year will hold until August of the next year is over. Decisions need to be made as much in response to crises as to the need for refinement and modification. A static state is a condition of evil and cannot be tolerated. Even good practices must be reviewed to allow for the renewal of their purposes and methods. Even the Good can decay because of a static state. The only growth state is the state of movement toward greater and greater perfection.

The School may decide to bring within its physical walls the change that is external to it, and to accommodate such change educationally. Here we could take the example of integration and see ways in which the School might devise programs for treating the subject whether or not it becomes involved in physical steps leading to integration. The whole subject of integration could become part of the Social Studies curriculum and could be used to look at the problems of contemporary society, or it could be used as a vehicle for students' leadership activities and their involvement in the affairs of minority groups. In other words, there are ways in which the School can decide to take a positive stand regarding elements of change and use these elements as educational material through exciting programmatic choices.

The School may decide to encourage change from within in order to seek constructive educational expression. For example, rather than waiting for change to confront it, the School may encourage the exploration of newer content, innovative instructional methods, and creative responses to the social world of change. The School can initiate from within and can openly challenge its teachers to inquire and to pursue such inquiry. Under such an approach the School might move into various kinds of administrative patterns such as team teaching or flexible scheduling. Or the School might move into curriculum content that is new to it—for instance Non-Western Studies or Sex Education. The School might move into new technology such as computerized instruction, or provisions for independent study for students, or sabbatical leaves for teachers, or the lengthening of the school day, or the utilization of the school building as a community center for adults. The point is that whether or not a thousand other schools have already taken the step becomes irrelevant. The relevant matter is recognizing that this one particular school has taken steps to move forward, that this one school has decided to move forward for itself because of itself, not for others or because of others. This too becomes leadership.

The School may decide to accept change as inevitable. This becomes a sort of ultimate step. It becomes a testimony bearing witness to the fact that change is a part of life and that the moral responsibility and indeed the obligation of the School is to accept such inevitabilities and to grow because of them, exerting leadership functions over them. Such a position means that the School moves away from self-protection, away from defensiveness, and becomes an acknowledged part of the universe that is in change. Then, through its acceptance of change, the School announces its intention to remain alert, aware of its need to assess the significance of change, committed to the process of studying the ways in which it can continuously respond to change, and professional in evaluating its self-directed recommendations for the implementation of change. Such a school is a school of and for society. It is a strong institution able to play a powerful role in changing society. It is not a weak institution crying that society is out to change it, crying that society is never satisfied and is always blaming it. Such a school is not paranoid. It is adult and it is wise. Such a school decides to design for change.

The School can challenge time through such an approach. It can rise from an era of doubt over its success and scepticism over its direction to a position in the vanguard of the social revolution sweeping the world. But it cannot do so with random or scattered efforts, with impotence or with resentment. Its only course is that of ordering change and interpreting it in terms of its functions as a school and of manifesting plans for projecting change into the vast spaces of time and place.

THE ELEMENTS

A design for change may be found in a process that builds upon itself and gives rise to a stable edifice representing faith in its foundations and pride in the prospect it presents for all to behold.

A design uses the knowledge resulting from the completion of the aforementioned tasks the School has set for itself. It is a conscious plan; it is based upon study; it is a choice made by the School as the one